Life Matters

How Grief and Horses Changed My Life

KATHRYN WHITE

Copyright

Cathean Publishing - in collaboration with Oxford Literary Consultancy

Cover Photo – courtesy of Candice Pottage Photography

Disclaimer
This book is a memoir based on the author's own life. Certain names and events have been changed to protect the privacy of individuals. Life Matters also recounts the author's experience of various alternative healing methods, but it is not intended as a substitute for medical advice. Readers should regularly consult their own physician with regard to health matters, especially if any symptoms may require diagnosis or medical attention.

Kathryn White
www.cathean.co.uk

Dedication

Dedicated to my darling Ian,
for opening my heart to love,
and to Moose, Willow and Wilbur
for the joy you brought into my life.
Team White rocked!

CONTENTS

Testimonials

An excellent and moving read.
S Brener, writer.

A truly inspirational account of Kathryn's journey through love, loss and healing, illustrating the strength of the human spirit. I'm both humbled and honoured to have been a small part in Kathryn's story and encourage anyone going through such a life changing experience to read it and to draw strength from it.
K Watson, My Own Coach

I couldn't put it down and finished it the day after I started it. I found it very easy to read, although obviously very emotional, but I also found it incredibly inspiring, open and honest. I salute you for your amazing ability to find the positives in a very negative situation. This book has broad appeal, but it will resonate particularly with anyone who has ever lost a loved one and is feeling totally heartbroken and lost, not knowing how or why to carry on, as well as with people who have a similar passion for horses and especially eventing.
L Fussey, Brain Tumour Research

Wonderfully well written and expressed, offering comfort as well as some practical advice and warnings of the pitfalls and traps that lie ahead after a bereavement. It is moving, poignant, but uplifting, too – a tribute to the power of love and a testament to the strength and fortitude of the human spirit.
K Bush, author

Life Matters has been written from the heart and soul. The result is a story that's deeply honest, very personal and intensely sad, yet incredibly inspiring at the same time.
Michelle Higgs, tutor, Writers Online

Foreword One

Most of us have to deal with bereavement at some point in our lives, but few of us have to deal with the loss of somebody close while they are in their prime, as in Kathryn's case.

I first met Ian and Kathryn when my horse was stabled at the livery yard where they were based. They were both experienced and bold eventers, while even in those days, I was a 'wussy' dressage rider. I well remember the Saturday morning that Kathryn came to me and asked if I could have a quick look at Ian. He had been to see his GP approximately two weeks beforehand, after he began to suffer from severe headaches and overwhelming tiredness. However, given his blood tests had been normal, he'd been prescribed strong painkillers.

Ian was not the type of person to make a fuss; nor would he go to see his GP unless there was something significantly wrong. As a psychiatrist, I was able to conduct a very simple neurological examination without any equipment and realised that Ian was not his normal self. It was very difficult to confirm what was wrong with him: he was just 'not Ian'. I advised Kathryn and Ian to go back to the GP and if the GP would not organise a brain scan, then I would. They did this, and the rest of Kathryn's story is described in this book.

Looking back on events, there were subtle changes to Ian's personality and behaviour about two months before Kathryn approached me.

I remember going to a dressage competition where Ian and I were in the same class so riding exactly the same test. Ian, to everybody's surprise, forgot the test and made a simple mistake, which should have cost him dearly. However, the judge didn't appear to notice the error and Ian finished on a better score than I did. On reflection, I think this was the first sign of subtle neurological changes. When I teach medical students, I often talk about listening to patients, as they have the answers. It sounds simplistic, but Ian's story seems to me to be an example of doctors not hearing what has been said to them.

Kathryn's journey has been long and hard, but her strength has been an inspiration to all those who are fortunate enough to know her and is a testament to her relationship with Ian. I hope you read this book and find it a source of interest, help and comfort.

Dr Neil Brener MBBS MRCPsych. Consultant Psychiatrist.

Foreword Two

I first met Kathryn in March 2015 when she came to a lunch we were holding to raise funds for Brain Tumour Research's annual Wear A Hat Day campaign. Kathryn was a young widow, yet was strong and positive; it's a strange and tragic disease that brings so many of us together.

We lost our beloved niece, Alison Phelan, in June 2001, three weeks before her eighth birthday. Inspired by Ali and angered by the lack of treatments, together with Ali's family and friends we set up the charity Ali's Dream to fund research into childhood brain tumours. Alongside fellow brain tumour charities, we launched the national charity Brain Tumour Research in 2009.

In Kathryn, I recognised the same determination to make a difference and stop others hurting as we had.

Life Matters is a story of strength over adversity and one which, sadly, many people will relate to.

Beginning with Kathryn's early years as a pony-obsessed child, the book tells of her early years before going to university and meeting Ian, who quickly became her soulmate. Later they married, believing this was happy-ever-after and that they would spend a glorious lifetime together. Ian quickly began to share Kathryn's passion for horses. He went on to buy his own horse, Moose, to whom he was soon totally devoted, and also got the bug for eventing. The happy couple spent many horsey weekends competing around the country. Ian was even awarded a rosette at Gatcombe Park by HRH Princess Anne.

Tragically, in 2008 Ian was diagnosed with a brain tumour, aged just 41.

Like far too many people, Ian was initially misdiagnosed for several months. Despite many visits to the GP as well as a trip to A&E because of his excruciating headaches and vomiting, and feelings of exhaustion, dizziness and confusion, these symptoms were attributed to migraine. The couple had to beg for Ian to be referred for a brain scan; they were left to feel that such scans were normally reserved for people with serious brain issues like tumours, not mere migraines. Heart-breakingly, I have heard too many stories like this.

Kathryn's anguish and frustration during what turned out to be just three months between Ian's diagnosis and his passing is sadly shared by too many families. I understand their sheer devastation when they were told that the tumour was inoperable and the only treatments on offer – radiotherapy and chemotherapy – would give him a few more months of precious life. How can this be in this day and age?

Brain tumours kill more children and adults under the age of 40 than any other cancer, yet just 1% of the national spend on cancer research has been allocated to this devastating disease. This is why for Ian, and the thousands of patients diagnosed each year with high-grade brain tumours, there is still no cure – and is why Brain Tumour Research is dedicated to funding sustainable research to improve outcomes for patients and their families.

The use of extracts from Kathryn's diary to give the reader insight into her emotional state, particularly during the months leading up to losing Ian, I found particularly poignant. It was lovely, however, to find that amongst the gloom and despair, the couple still found lots of things to laugh about – including Ian's night-time call for help from his hospital bed.

As Ian became increasingly ill, Kathryn initially baulked at the thought of having him transferred to a hospice rather than dying at home. I was glad to read that she was unexpectedly surprised and hugely comforted by the experience. The staff at the Sue Ryder hospice in Nettlebed do their utmost to make this sad time as comfortable and uplifting as possible for both patients and their families. They even allowed Ian's beloved Moose (the hospice's first ever equine visitor) to come and see Ian during his last days.

But losing Ian isn't where the story ends. After an agonisingly difficult period, Kathryn describes what she has done to help herself move on from being a grief-stricken widow to someone who can now experience joy and beauty in her life again, but still with the memories of her beloved Ian. She shares with the reader the strategies and techniques she has found helpful in rebuilding her life. She tells how a dog and horses have helped in her healing, as well as spirituality and alternative therapies like Reiki and quantum energy healing. Such techniques might not be for everyone, but may offer food for thought and hope for others who find themselves in similar circumstances.

I was inspired by reading Kathryn's book. It is a real love story in which she shares her highs and lows before and after losing Ian with openness and honesty. You can't fail to feel her emotion or be left feeling empowered by Kathryn's positive way of facing the challenges of her life.

When we set up Brain Tumour Research back in 2009 we had a vision of finding a cure, and a mission to build a network of experts in sustainable brain tumour research. Our aim was to establish seven dedicated research centres and to campaign to increase the national spend on brain tumour research to £30-£35 million a year. With the help of our member charities, fundraising groups and supporters like Kathryn, I am pleased to say we have already established four Centres of Excellence (within Imperial College, London, Queen Mary University of

London, The University of Portsmouth and Plymouth University) and are working towards a fifth.

What's more, following a successful e-petition started by Maria Lester and her family, signed by over 120,000 people, a petitions committee report and a Westminster Hall debate attended by over 70 MPs, a Department of Health Task and Finish Group Working Party was established to increase the level and impact of research into brain tumours. Brain Tumour Research has been proud to play a leading role in this working party, and we are pleased that initiatives are already being announced.

Whatever journey you are on, thank you for reading this book, for supporting Kathryn and for supporting our work.

Together we will find a cure.

Sue Farrington Smith, MBE, Chief Executive, Brain Tumour Research
www.braintumourresearch.org

Acknowledgements

Sincere thanks to my mentor and editor, Stephanie Hale of Oxford Literary Consultancy, for believing in my story and my ability to tell it. Your encouragement – and patience – particularly when self-doubt pervaded, are much appreciated.

Thank you to Jacqueline Broderick and her team at Lavender and White Publishing for additional editing services and to everyone who very kindly read early drafts of the manuscript to give me their feedback and testimonials.

Thank you to Michelle, my tutor during the home study courses I've completed with Writers Online, for your positive and constructive critique on all my assignments and this book. Your faith in me as a writer gave me the courage to submit articles to magazines for publication and started the ball rolling for publishing this book.

Thank you to Steve Cripps, graphic designer extraordinaire, for your artistic wizardry, and Lisa Hughes for your marketing expertise.

Thank you Kevin, Elaine, Dawn, Pam and Louise for helping me discover the 'real Kathryn' and for all the lightbulb moments – not to mention the tears and laughter – we've shared along the way. My life today is testament to the power of counselling and therapy.

Thanks to Alex Wade of Reviewed & Cleared for legal advice.

Finally, I would not be where I am today without the incredible love and friendship of my beautiful, generous, kind – and crazy – mates. Thank you for making my life so much fun.

Prologue

A good friend of mine likened the process of grief to peeling layers of an onion. Not that the grief diminishes, it's just that with each phase, or layer, you learn something new and move on. For anyone going through the loss of a life partner, whether it be through bereavement or divorce, it is a significant and traumatic event that shatters your life, future and self-confidence into tiny, heart-wrenching fragments.

In 2008, my husband Ian tragically died just nine weeks after being diagnosed with a high-grade brain tumour. He was 41 years old.

There is nothing like a tragedy to force you to re-evaluate your life. Widowed at 37 and overwhelmed, I had an overriding desire to live the life I had dreamt of as a young child to honour Ian's life and the dreams he never got to fulfil.

I haven't made it through these years following Ian's demise without a lot of help from family, friends and professionals. Horses have been a fundamental part of my life, from being a pony-obsessed youngster desperate to have riding lessons to a 30-year old adult, finally owning my own horse.

Ian and I shared a passion for equestrianism. We enjoyed several years of horse ownership and competed against top riders in the sport of eventing. These beautiful animals will always have a special place in my heart and have even played a part in my recovery.

Life isn't easy. Change is inevitable. Challenges are par for the course. I still have my fair share of wobbly days when I want to scream and yell at the unfairness of it all; to remain within the safety of my duvet and weep. It's all part of the process of peeling another layer of that damn shallot.

If you have picked this book up because you have faced bereavement or loss, I truly hope that my story provides you some confidence that good can come out of the blackness. Grief is very much a personal process – there is no right and wrong – and you have to take the path that's right for you. Have the strength and courage to accept help when needed and, most importantly of all, be kind to yourself. If you have chosen to read *Life Matters* out of interest, then my message to you is to follow your heart in whatever you do in life.

Part One

Horses Come Between Toys and Boys

Chapter 1
My connection with horses begins

The deep dark water stretches out in front me; small ripples reveal the slight breeze. I sit on one of the cold grey kerbstones bordering the grassy path which snakes its way around the reservoir. I let my legs dangle freely over the side and swirl my feet in circles like I did when a child.

My companion is a small scruffy black terrier, who sits close beside me, keeping a keen eye on the ducks gently bobbing along. As I look into the depths below, my mind wanders and wonders: how did I end up being married, let alone widowed?

As a child, and much to my mum's despair, I was resolute in my decision never to be wed. My future was all planned out. I would live alone on a remote farm, surrounded by the glorious British countryside with my horse, cat, dog and canary - random, I know, but this chirpy yellow bird always featured on my list. It seemed I was destined to become an eccentric hermit.

They say that horses keep you young: they fill the gap between toys and boys. That was certainly true for me and I was your typical horse-obsessed child. Duvet cover, lampshade, curtains – you name it – I had horses plastered all over. Where the walls weren't covered in horsey wallpaper, I attached photos ripped out of magazines or pictures created by me – my own attempt at equestrian artwork. Even the books on my shelf all had one thing in common: the horse.

One of the happiest days of my life remains the time when Dad finally relented, worn down by persistent pleas, and booked me onto my first riding lesson.

In a village nestled at the foot of Pendle Hill, surrounded by spectacular moorland, Fence Riding School was my haven from the age of 11. I enjoyed weekly riding lessons aboard horses and ponies of various shapes, sizes and ages, all with gloriously quirky characters that helped them cope with the myriad of children of varying abilities whom they taught to ride.

From day one, I felt at home here among the old-fashioned brick stables, the stalls with polished mahogany partitions, the cobbled yard and a tack room that smelled of leather mingled with tobacco.

Despite only ever having sat on the back of a beach donkey before, I instantly felt at home aboard one of the smallest residents of the riding school, Twinkle. A 13.2 hh chestnut and rotund pony, she had a mass of ginger mane which sprouted in all directions and a tail that almost touched the ground. I had devoured every book on stable management and riding so I knew the theory. I loved having the opportunity to put what I knew into practice. I had a lot of fun riding Twinkle, though she kept her party trick to herself until the end of the lesson.

I turned her towards the centre of the school, where there was a vertical metal girder wrapped with old sacking from the floor to about shoulder height. I closed my hands around the reins to give the signal to halt, but Twinkle had other ideas. She sidled close to this post, turned her hairy bottom towards it and began rubbing her tail against the rough hessian sacks. She grunted in delight as she satisfied her itch while I swayed left and right, gripping onto the front of the saddle with both hands.

Thankfully, after a couple of minutes she stopped, but that wasn't the end. As I let go of the pommel and took my feet out of the stirrups, she gave an almighty shake, like a dog ridding itself of excess water. Off I flew, sideways, landing in a heap beside her on the soft sandy ground of the arena. Not quite the dismount I had studied in my books, but I did see the funny side.

This little incident didn't put me off, either; I was hooked.

It didn't take long for me to become a more frequent visitor than once a week and I spent many a happy school holiday mucking out and caring for the equine residents in return for free riding lessons.

While most of my friends were pursuing boys or having crushes on the latest pop star, I was chasing an errant pony around a paddock, squelching through mud in an attempt to entice him into a warm stable or reading about my equestrian heroes in the latest edition of *Horse and Pony Magazine*.

I wasn't alone in my obsession. A group of similar-aged, like-minded girls hung out at the yard with me. We competed at the village gymkhana on the riding school ponies and, once a year, dressed up for the riding club's award evening at the local pub. A real treat was riding the horses, unescorted by the yard staff, along the winding lanes that took us up onto the hills. Cantering along the grassy bridleways and splashing through the streams that bubble and gurgle their way through that landscape, I felt free. Being on horseback gave me a feeling of independence. At school, I was an outsider, never accepted by the various cliques, but when I was with the horses, outdoors in the fresh air and countryside, I felt a sense of belonging that I didn't feel anywhere else.

I don't know where this love of all things equine came from. None of my family is remotely interested in horses. The only equestrian link I can think of was through my maternal granddad, Harry, who enjoyed a weekly bet on racehorses. I loved watching the racing on TV with him. We'd sit in my grandparents' living room, in front of the glowing heat of the gas fire, which was always on whatever the weather, with the obligatory butter dish warming underneath. I would sit on his knee so he could jog me up and down as if I was riding, lifting me over the imaginary fences while I laughed with sheer delight.

Granddad and I once travelled to the nearby coastal town of Blackpool to see the legendary racehorse, and multiple Grand National winner, Red Rum, who was on tour around the UK. Quite a crowd turned up to see him, but somehow Granddad and I managed to find our way to the front and there, inches away from me, was this magnificent thoroughbred horse. I held out my hand to touch the velvety smooth hair of this beautiful champion, with his muscles rippling under the shine of his coat. I felt in awe at meeting this equine hero of mine, a poster of whom had pride of place on my bedroom wall. He seemed huge – his legs were taller than me! I remember not wanting to wash my hands for the rest of that day.

Being around horses was, and remains, my refuge, my escape. They resonate with my soul, the very core of my being. It's like when you meet someone for the first time, or join a group of people, and you instantly feel at home with them, as if there's already a connection. Well, whenever I'm around horses, I feel I belong; I feel grounded and content around them. It's as if my airways untangle and I can suddenly breathe more easily. Despite the absence of any significant equine connection within my family, horses feel familiar to me, like my soul remembers that these incredible, spiritual beings are a part of my tribe from a past life.

My thoughts would frequently drift off to the rural idyll I created in my imagination. I was a shy child who lacked any self-confidence so these daydreams were a means of escaping stress and any teenage angst. I think it's safe to say I got on with horses better than people.

I was a conscientious student at school and did well; in my spare time, bus fares to the stables took most of my pocket money so I was one of the few kids thankful for a uniform – I had no money for, and little interest in, fashion. As a consequence, life at school could be a little challenging.

A few of us from my year and a small group of older students were chosen to go on a week-long writing course at Lumb Bank, a former home of poet laureate Ted Hughes. The granite-stone farmhouse, with its mullion windows, stood on the side of a hill overlooking the wild West Yorkshire moors which rose up from the market town of Hebden Bridge. This is a landscape steeped in literary heritage, with the Brontë sisters in nearby Haworth, and I felt the creative vibe strongly as words flowed with ease from my head onto paper.

Each morning our tutors gave us a theme for the day and then we were allowed to wander around the gardens and nearby village to seek inspiration and create our masterpieces. In the evenings, the two resident authors would select some of our stories or poems to be read out to the group while we all sat on the large leather sofas, soaking up the heat from the roaring open fire.

One evening I was feeling a little under the weather so retired to bed early. We slept in bunk beds in dormitories sleeping about five of us. I undressed and slipped under the covers of my bottom bunk, thankful to rest my head on the soft pillow. I do not know how long I had been there before I heard the unmistakable creak of the dormitory door opening. My bedside light was on so the rest of the girls could find their way when they came upstairs later. Soft footsteps padded past me accompanied by whispered voices. I held my breath and kept my eyes firmly shut, thankful that I was facing the wall so no-one could tell whether I was asleep or not.

"Click, click!"

A suitcase was opened.

"Oh, God! Have you seen this?" someone whispered excitedly as others tried to stifle their giggles.

"I think her grandma knitted it. Look, it has a mane, too," said another.

My heart sank. It was my suitcase. They were rooting through my belongings and had found the woollen jumper that, yes, Grandma had kindly made for me, beautifully knitted with a horse's head on the front. It was, as a 13-year old, my favourite piece of clothing.

"I wouldn't be seen dead wearing that," sniggered someone.

"What are you doing?" asked a stern voice.

One of the older girls had entered the room. I heard my suitcase being closed and the gaggle of girls was ushered out.

I couldn't contain my tears any longer and a loud sob erupted from under my duvet.

"I'm so sorry, Kathryn. Are you OK?" asked the same voice, as she gently placed her hand on my shoulder.

Shock and disappointment rendered me motionless.

"It's OK. I've got your back from now on," she soothed before she left, turning off the bedside light and closing the door behind her, plunging the room into darkness.

True to her word, this lovely person looked after me for the rest of that week. Despite this incident, I thoroughly enjoyed my time on that writers' retreat and fully immersed myself in the therapeutic word flow that came from being there.

A couple of years later, I left the all-girls' school for the more mature and sociable environment of a co-ed tertiary college to study A-levels. University beckoned. I realised from those idyllic days of helping out at the riding school that an equestrian career wasn't for me. I wanted to earn sufficient money to buy my own horses and ride for pleasure so I studied hard, and an interest in boys and socialising with friends replaced that of equine pursuits.

Chapter 2
Childhood dreams are challenged

L eaving home and heading off to Nottingham University was the making of me. I finally achieved the independence I had craved as a child. I could come and go as I pleased. Everything was within walking distance from where I lived or accessible via public transport. I felt liberated! I threw myself into university life and, though I studied hard, enjoyed the social aspects of living on campus among my fellow scholars in halls of residence.

Unbeknownst to me at the time, fate was already playing its part in my destiny because it was during the first term of my second year that the unexpected happened. The plans I'd carefully made during childhood were challenged when I met my future husband.

Ian and I lived in Willoughby Hall on campus during our first year, so I knew of him, but our social circles had never crossed. I often saw him in the evenings waiting for his friends in the entrance hall, wearing a light brown leather flying jacket. I thought he was good-looking, but there was no obvious spark there. Besides, I was enjoying student life and the freedom I felt. Why would I want to encumber myself with a relationship? However, the Universe had other ideas, as had a mutual friend of ours, Sam, a fellow resident.

"I have a mate, Ian, who's recently split up with his girlfriend," Sam explained with a cheeky smile on his face as we sat having a drink in the bar one evening.

"Yes, I know who he is. I'm really not interested," I replied. "I'm happy on my own, thank you very much, and I don't need Cupid creating any complications right now."

I hadn't done as well as I had wanted to in my first-year exams so knew I had to improve my marks to achieve the level of degree I had set my sights on – first class honours.

Sam sighed. "OK, well why don't you just come and play volleyball with us on Wednesday night – no pressure?" he promised.

I gave him a sideways glance and grunted. "OK, but no matchmaking."

There was no harm in going out with him and his friend and I was under no obligation to turn anything into a romance.

Wednesday evening came and Sam and I headed off to the sports centre together to meet Ian, who was now living off campus in student digs.

We entered the brightly lit sports hall where an alarmingly high net divided the volleyball court in half. My stomach lurched with nerves. I had never played volleyball before and, looking around, I didn't know anyone apart from Sam and Ian.

"Oh great!" I thought. "Let's hope I don't make a complete fool of myself."

Having been introduced to Ian, clearly a man of few words as he barely said hello, I timidly followed him and Sam onto the court as the teams assembled. Everyone else looked highly competent and I swallowed nervously as I took up my position. I survived the first few minutes of that match by skilfully (I thought) avoiding the ball. All that was to change when it was my turn to serve. There was no hiding now. I took a deep breath, threw the ball in the air and smacked it as hard as I could with my hand. Whack! The ball hit the net. One chance gone.

The same thing happened the second time and my face was flaming with embarrassment. This was my third and final serve and I didn't want to give points away. Saying a silent prayer, I gave the ball a good hard wallop out of desperation and watched in utter amazement as the orange orb sailed magnificently over the net. Clearly taken by surprise, our opponents stood still, faces agog, as the ball hit the ground within the court. I scored an ace.

Despite going back to training a couple more times, my skills didn't improve. Volleyball clearly wasn't my forté, but those sessions served their purpose because afterwards, Sam, Ian and I would go to one of the bars on campus for a drink.

We were nothing more than friends at this stage – in fact, I wouldn't even go as far as that because Ian seemed to spend most of the time ignoring me and speaking to everyone else. That is, until the end-of-term Christmas party, December 1990.

Snow was imminent as Sam and I made our way out into the dark, heads bowed against the bitter biting wind to walk across the parkland. We were going to meet friends at the disco over in Sherwood Hall. We pulled our coats firmly around us as snowflakes began spiralling their way to the ground in front of us, dancing in the bright lights that shone out to greet us. It was a relief to get to our destination and be hugged by the warm air inside. The infectious 'end-of-term' atmosphere was catching and it didn't take long for us to discard our coats, grab a drink and join in with the dancing.

"Is Ian coming to the party?" I shouted in Sam's ear, desperately trying to be heard above the thumping music.

He bent down to catch what I was saying and shrugged his shoulders in response. Why was I suddenly so interested in Mr White's attendance? I had not been aware of any feelings for him to date. So why did I have butterflies in my stomach and why did I keep glancing over at the door?

Then my heart fluttered, taking me once more by surprise, as there he was. In walked Ian flanked by two male friends. But wait. A pretty blonde appeared in front of him and, with a big grin, threw her arms around him. My heart felt like it was hanging in anticipation and I felt compelled to keep watching. Throwing her head back with laughter, she led him over to her friends on the dance floor. I inhaled deeply and let out a long sigh. Ah well! He was clearly already taken. I tore my eyes away from them, turned my back and carried on dancing, but I couldn't shake the feeling of disappointment.

A few moments later, I felt Sam's eyes boring into me. He was gesturing at me to look round. Ian was heading over! I quickly turned my gaze back to our group and closed my eyes. My heart soared to a whole new level of giddiness.

"Stay upright," I instructed myself under my breath. "Stay calm."

We all greeted each other and Ian introduced us to his two friends, who were visiting from home.

"Who's the blonde then?" teased Sam.

"She's just a friend!" laughed Ian. "She's on my course."

Sam turned towards me and gave me a sneaky wink before pushing his way through the crowd to get some more drinks.

Ian and his friends stayed dancing with us for the remainder of the night. Absorbed in the music and the vibe of the party, I lost track of time until the DJ announced the penultimate song – Love Shack, by the B52s, the student anthem for that year. That tune still brings back fond memories of my university days. I willed my tired, aching legs to keep moving to the energetic beat. In that moment, I felt incredibly content. Here I was, having fun, surrounded by great mates and with the prospect of time off from studying and lectures for a whole three weeks.

Could my life get any better?

"Follow me," said a voice in my ear, and I turned to see Ian beside me.

He took my hand in his and pulled me gently towards him. I willingly complied as tingles fizzed round my body like an electric current zipping through my veins.

"Come on," he said.

I didn't need asking twice. He led me out into the entrance hall, where people were already gathering and saying goodbye to each other. Instinctively, we turned to face each other and kissed. Oh, he was a great kisser! So gentle and light, like a whisper on my lips.

"Er. Hmm."

A gruff voice penetrated our bubble and I leapt back, feeling somewhat embarrassed.

"Mate, can't you see I'm busy?" Ian said, turning back towards me.

But the security guard, weary from a night of student shenanigans, wanted to get home and wasn't putting up with Ian's cheek. We were shown out into the now snowy grounds. Despite the freezing cold air swirling around us, I felt insulated by a warm glow that came from within me.

Ian drew me close again for a goodnight kiss before running to catch up with his mates, leaving Sam and me to walk home, with me still giddy from my first romantic encounter with Mr White.

I thought that would be that, a one-night event, but the next afternoon Ian rang me and said he'd come over for a drink. We met in the hall bar where I was sitting with a few friends whom Ian already knew from being a resident himself the previous year.

He sat down beside me and placed his arm around my waist, tucking his hand into the rear pocket of my jeans. Once more, my body buzzed from his touch and at that moment, I felt the luckiest girl in the room.

The bar became busier and the clientele more raucous as the night progressed so Ian suggested we found a quieter place to chat. We made our excuses and walked out amidst a chorus of wolf whistles from our mates, to find refuge in the empty common room.

I felt like we had known each other for years. He was good looking, with his boyish features and kindly brown eyes which sparkled with mischief whenever he smiled. Although he wasn't much taller than me, his broad muscular shoulders and chest made me feel safe and secure when he wrapped his arms around me. He had a great sense of humour and, unlike with the few boys I had dated before, I felt a deep connection between us. I loved chatting to him about life; putting the world to rights. It seemed we shared similar views and beliefs and I felt completely at ease in his company.

I knew from the beginning that this was the real deal. Furthermore, at 23, he was four years older than me and classed as a mature student – an oxymoron if ever I heard one. I could not believe my luck: a gorgeous 'older man' had fallen for me, the class swot, the plain Jane.

That night he stayed over in my room, rather than staggering the few miles home. He was a complete gentleman, though more than a few eyebrows were raised the next morning as we walked hand in hand past the dining hall on our way to lectures.

Chapter 3
Love and challenges

A week or so after we met, it was the end of autumn term. Ian and I went our separate ways to spend Christmas with our families, but Ian travelled north to stay with my parents and me up in Lancashire for the New Year. My mum and dad enjoyed his company and Dad loved discussing current affairs and football with him. In fact, the three of us went to several football matches together whenever Tottenham Hotspur (Ian's team) played Blackburn Rovers (Dad's team) over the years we were together.

After spending a few days in the north west, we drove south together so that I could meet his parents, whom I instantly fell in love with. His mum, Pat, and I hit it off straight away; she was a fellow horse lover so we had plenty in common.

Their home, Parkview, was my idea of a countryside idyll. Situated down a single-track leafy lane in deepest rural Berkshire, this beautiful but humble home had views over rolling fields flanked by tall majestic trees and hedgerows. Pheasants strutted their way through the apple orchard and rabbits bobbed into view and disappeared just as quickly.

Pat made the best Sunday roast, often accompanied by home-grown vegetables. Her blackcurrant crumble, made with no additional sugar, was so tart that your first mouthful always made you scrunch your eyes and purse your lips. It was best served with a dollop of her home-made velvety rich ice cream to soften the sharpness. More often than not, Ian and I were sent home with leftovers such as her legendary rum-soaked trifle or delicious raspberry cream slices. Ian's gran lived here, too, and after lunch we would take the family dog for a walk round the fields before heading to Granny's flat to play cards and hear tales of her youth. She was great company and a lot of fun; a lady with a wicked sense of humour and an infectious giggle.

Over time, Parkview became a place where I felt at home and at peace.

Ian rarely told me he loved me, but his actions spoke volumes and I never doubted how he felt about me. On birthdays and anniversaries, I'd receive flowers and on my 21st, he prepared a delicious three course meal for us, much to the amusement of his housemates, who were all convinced he was going to propose.

He was a fantastic cook and had set up a table for two in his room, resplendent with flowers and candles.

"Dear diary, I managed a trip to Reading despite my studies. Ian said he'd go mad if he didn't see me soon. I travelled down by train so I could revise, and felt so excited about seeing him again. He looked really good in his flying jacket when he met me at the station. My heart missed a beat. It is the first time I have felt this way about anyone. On the train ride home, I found a little note in my purse saying, 'I'll love you always, Ian'. Wow! I couldn't feel more loved. I'm feeling much more motivated about my exams now."

Ian was also a very practical person, proficient at house, garden and car maintenance. He had enjoyed tinkering around with old cars as a teenager and he brought the same attention to detail to all the jobs he did. I'll never forget the look on his mum's face when he asked for a bath panel – yes, the side of a bath – for his birthday, along with a garden fork, after he bought his first house in Nottingham. That story became a White family legend.

Ian had integrity in spades. There were no sides to him. What you saw was what you got. He was a private person, never one to be centre of attention, but when he got to know you and if he liked you, he was a very loyal and sincere friend; a great person to have on your side. Ian was great fun when he was with people he knew and liked, but put him in a situation where he didn't feel comfortable and he would become very quiet and withdrawn or irritable. If he didn't like you, he wouldn't have anything to do with you. It was that black and white.

This could prove tricky at times.

I recall one party my friends and I hosted at our student house during my early months as a postgraduate, still at Nottingham University. Ian had recently started his first job at a manufacturing plant, also located in Nottingham, so though we were physically located in the same place, our lives were diverging as we began new phases of our lives.

At some point during that evening, I became aware that Ian had disappeared. I picked my way through the pockets of people chatting, dancing and drinking. No sign of him anywhere and no-one seemed to have seen him for a while, either. I began to worry. Had he gone home? Would he leave without saying goodbye to me first? I went to my room upstairs, wondering whether to give his housemates a call. I opened the door and there he was, curled up on my bed, facing the wall.

"What are you doing up here?" I asked, softly, carefully sitting down beside him.

"I'm fine," he replied, with a hint of irritation in his voice. "You carry on, leave me here."

Was he unwell?

"No, honestly, I'm fine," he insisted, and curled up tighter.

I couldn't leave it. I was crushed that he didn't want to spend time with me and my new friends. "Come on! You're missing a great party," I implored.

"They're not my crowd; I'm not a student anymore. Please go downstairs and enjoy yourself. I really am fine up here."

Saddened and disappointed by his unwillingness to embrace my friends, I sighed and got up. I desperately wanted him to like my friends and be sociable. Of course, I spent the rest of the evening worrying about the situation.

Meeting so young and at university meant our relationship survived many of these sorts of challenges as we accompanied each other through life's transitions, evolving from being students to finding our first jobs. Though I found Ian's moods difficult to handle at times, I could not have asked for an otherwise more attentive and loyal partner.

To be fair, being with me presented its own problems. I was naïve where romantic relationships were concerned. My love of horses had kept me young – spending time at the stables rather than out on the town getting drunk with my friends. Being at an all-girls school hadn't helped my social skills where the opposite sex was concerned, either. Looking back, I can see how irresponsible I was, too, in the sense that I let Ian take responsibility for all the decisions we made during our time together. That way, if anything went wrong, I couldn't be to blame, I suppose.

As Ian had worked as an apprentice engineer before deciding to pursue a more academic route, his friends were very different to mine. They were all working, settling down with their partners and getting married.

I recall the first time I went out drinking with Ian and his friends around the bars and clubs in the centre of Reading. I dressed up in my usual 'going out' clothes, which was the typical student uniform of that time: denim shorts, thick black tights and Doc Marten boots. Judging by the reaction I got from the nightclub bouncers, my outfit didn't meet the dress code for this particular establishment. It took some persuasion by Ian and his friends to get me inside.

After the embarrassment of not being accepted at the door, I tried hard to fit in with the rest of the group. Consequently, I went home a little the worse for wear, having drunk several bottles of strong cider rather than my usual pints of bitter. I collapsed into bed that night with the room spinning around me.

At some point in the early hours, I awoke with a thumping head and desperate for the toilet. Ian and I were staying at his parents so slept in separate rooms. I slowly opened my bedroom door and crept along the landing to the bathroom. All was going well until I began my return journey, back along the corridor. Two closed doors were in front of me, but in my alcohol-induced haze I couldn't remember which one was mine. I did know, however, that behind one of them slept Ian's mum and dad. I stood, swaying in the dark, as the doors in front of me went in and out of focus, mocking my drunken stupor. Mercifully for me and his parents, I chose the right one and didn't emerge from under the duvet until close to lunchtime.

Despite our different backgrounds, Ian and I had a very strong bond and respect for each other. This deep affection saw us through the many twists and turns of life. We were still growing up and establishing ourselves in the world. Regardless, I knew early on, and despite my reservations about marriage, that he was the man I wanted to be with for the rest of my life.

Chapter 4
Horses, friends and family fun

It wasn't long before horses became a shared passion of ours. Although Ian's mum was a fellow horsewoman, her son didn't share her interest in horses when he was a child, preferring to climb trees than jump on a pony.

I believe he once turned up at the local riding school in his slippers, such was his enthusiasm for riding. Pat, however, was a fully-fledged horse nut and owned a fabulous chestnut gelding called Guinea when we first met. A qualified riding instructor, she kindly let me ride Guinea whenever Ian and I visited their family home, and I enjoyed being with her and their black Labrador, Zoe, at the stables. This was the stuff of childhood dreams. United by the same sense of humour, as well as sharing similar relationship challenges given the men we were with, Pat and I developed a strong bond. My future mother-in-law became a dear friend and always treated me like a daughter.

Knowing my love for horses, Ian realised early on in our partnership that he would have to learn to ride in order to spend any quality time with his girlfriend. So, during holidays from university, he asked his mum to give him lessons on Guinea.

After a while, his improving ability enabled us to go pony trekking during our first holiday together when we toured the north of England. I have fond memories of that ride across the North Yorkshire Moors and it was the turning point for Ian – the moment he realised his new-found love of riding.

We were a group of about 11 and Ian, being the only bloke, was given the weight-bearing plod who seemed very content to amble along at the back of the ride. We set off, the sound of horses' hooves thudding on the old turf beneath us. It was blissful! I rode beside Ian to make sure he was OK, but we soon found ourselves quite a way behind the others.

"Let's have a canter here!" yelled our trek leader.

This was clearly a known spot for having a pipe opener, as the horses were already jig-jogging in anticipation – all, that is, except Ian's, who seemed oblivious of the excitement ahead. The rest of the group set off, leaving us behind, eating their dust. Despite his best efforts, Ian's horse was resolutely staying in walk.

"Yell in his ear and kick harder," I suggested as my horse snatched at her bit and walked sideways, keen to follow her friends who were fast disappearing into the distance.

Wallop! That did it – off Ian went, laughing like a lunatic, a loud hearty guffaw of joy, as he was thrown momentarily backwards with the change of speed before grabbing hold of the front of the saddle and regaining his balance.

"Woohoo!" he shouted as he leant forward like a jockey.

I eased the pressure on my reins and my horse responded, leaping forward into a canter. We soon caught up with the rest of our group and enjoyed a thrilling and exhilarating gallop across the fields. That was it; Ian was hooked. When we returned home later in the week, he booked himself into his local stables to begin regular lessons.

After I'd ridden Guinea a few times in the paddock, Pat suggested I took him out around the lanes close by. The plan was that she and Ian would drive the route in the car and meet me at pre-designated places so they could point me in the right direction to the next meet-up point. I have to confess that as I got older and the roads had got steadily busier, I wasn't the bravest of riders when out hacking, but these were quiet leafy lanes and I trusted Pat's judgement; she was well aware of the risks and I knew she wouldn't have let just anyone take Guinea out.

All was going well until we arrived at the penultimate meeting place. Guinea and I made our way down the narrow country lane flanked by blackthorn hedgerows to where Pat and Ian had parked up in a convenient field gateway. As Guinea amiably clip-clopped along, I enjoyed the view from his back over the fields beyond. It was springtime, so crops were beginning to cover the brown earth with their green keenness of growth and the dainty white blooms of cow parsley danced in the light breeze, bringing the grassy banks alive beside us.

As we reached the car, Pat pointed her finger towards a grass verge that ran alongside a dual carriageway – the local bypass – running underneath the lane where we now stood. She explained that I could guide Guinea down the bank to our left.

"You can then canter him along the grassy strip beside the road and when you reach the next bridge, follow the track up the bank and onto the adjacent lane." She and Ian would meet me at the crossroads a little further along. "He loves cantering here, so enjoy."

It seemed simple enough, but our proximity to the bypass worried me. The roar of traffic seemed menacing, with the vehicles hurtling along the tarmac at speed.

"I can do this," I whispered to myself as we picked our way through the long grass to the track.

Guinea was clearly keen to get home and was getting somewhat impatient with our slow pace thus far. He jogged sideways, tossing his head up and down, snorting like a dragon possessed. I took a deep breath and squeezed my calves into his sides as a signal to canter. He obediently obliged, but when I lightened my weight in the saddle, he took full advantage and had his own fun.

With a squeal of delight, he bucked, kicking up his back heels and completely taking me by surprise. I somehow managed to regain my balance, but my hands slipped and the reins lengthened by an inch or two. That was enough for Guinea to take control and off he went at a headlong gallop. I grasped at the reins and desperately tugged on them to slow him down, but my attempts were futile. I had no brakes. Guinea was in charge and he was going home for his supper. The more I pulled, the stronger and faster he got.

As a horse rider, you're taught the importance of remaining calm at all times because the horse can pick up on your fear. Ha! I knew the theory, but the reality was that I was scared out of my wits and in no position to hide my feelings from Guinea. As my heart raced, so did he. The wind whistled past my ears as we sprinted alongside the traffic. I clung on for dear life as he swerved up the bank by the bridge that crossed the bypass. His sat nav had kicked in – he was on a mission and I was a mere passenger. All I could do was steer and hope we arrived back at the stables alive.

The single-track lane we emerged onto was mercifully quiet of traffic, but in the distance, a woman was walking her dog. I groaned. Her peace was about to be well and truly shattered.

Amidst the clattering of Guinea's hooves on the tarmac, I yelled, "Get out of my way, I can't stop!"

Oh, the embarrassment I felt as she scrambled up the grassy incline that flanked the lane. She was on all fours, grappling to keep her dog under control as it strained at his leash, barking with excitement, desperate to join in the race as Guinea and I sped by.

My mind flashed back to another time I was galloping out of control, on a little grey called Snip whom I adored. He was one of the riding school ponies and we had just won a rosette in the Family Pony class. Our lap of victory quickly became out of control as Snip, clearly buoyed by his success, and in a very non-'family pony'-like fashion, headed out of the ring at full pelt, scattering spectators like skittles as we hurtled up the showground.

"Competitors, DO NOT GALLOP around the show field," boomed the unmistakable voice of Dot, the formidable, larger-than-life owner of Fence Riding

School and show commentator. My cheeks burned red with humiliation and exertion as I pulled with all my might to control my delinquent mount.

I was jolted back to the moment as Guinea slipped. The road surface wasn't the best for his metal shoes. This did nothing to ease my nerves, but at least it meant he slowed down. I frantically yanked at his reins once more, pulled him onto the grass verge and leapt off his back as he floundered about trying to stay upright. I held tightly onto the bridle as he got himself together and stood beside me, panting.

He was dripping with sweat. White foam covered most of his hot clammy neck and his sides heaved in and out as he recovered his breath. Despite his appearance, his ears were perky and pricked and he chewed on the bit in his mouth as if eager to go again.

His eyes sparkled with energy and I'm sure that if he could have, he'd have said, "Now, that was exciting – fabulous gallop, don't you think?"

I wish I could have agreed, but to this day my knees have never knocked as they did then. My breaths were coming in quick rasping bursts and I was trembling from head to foot. I didn't know whether to laugh or cry at my predicament when I caught sight of Pat. She was on the bridge, looking back the way we had just come, clearly wondering where we had got to.

"Over here," I squeaked, my voice shaky and high-pitched from shock.

She waved acknowledgement and ran towards me with Ian close behind her.

"Oh, thank goodness you're OK," she said, giving me a big hug.

What a wonderful lady Pat was, clearly more concerned about my safety than whether her cherished horse was in one piece. It's always best to get back on a horse as soon as possible after a fall otherwise you risk permanently losing your confidence. After ensuring Guinea and I were OK, Pat hoisted me into the saddle and insisted I walked him home.

Sadly, Pat's much beloved Guinea was put to sleep a few years later, following a short illness. His replacement was the tricky and complex Mulberry, who I think must have had an unhappy past. This manifested itself in his many insecurities, particularly when ridden, some of which proved infuriating while others were just plain dangerous.

I have to hand it to her: Pat was one plucky woman and, despite the daily challenges she faced, she persevered with Mulberry and even took him along to local jumping and dressage competitions.

On one such day, she was competing at her local riding club Christmas show, a fancy dress event. Ian and I offered to get Mulberry ready for her while she added the final touches to her outfit – a string of tinkling bells. I know, I know. Not, perhaps, the best choice when riding any horse and particularly not one like Mulberry. Ian held onto the bridle as his mum mounted and lowered herself carefully onto the saddle, keeping the bells as quiet as possible. Mulberry flicked an ear back to acknowledge her presence but stood still.

"Good boy," soothed Ian, stroking the arched muscled neck beside him. "Are you OK?" he asked, looking up at his mum.

She nodded, but as Mulberry took a step forward the bells began to jangle. It was all too much for this nervy creature, who took off up the field, bucking and squealing as he went. How Pat stayed on I do not know, but all Ian and I could hear was her screeching "It's the bells! It's the bells!" as she galloped into the distance on her rodeo'ing steed.

I am afraid Ian and I were of no use whatsoever because we were doubled up in laughter while Pat expertly gained control of the snorting beast beneath her. Fair play to her: having removed the blasted bells, she went to the show and had a fun day.

Yes, horses gave us some of our most precious and fun times together as a family. In Pat, as in Ian, I found someone who was on my wavelength, with common values and beliefs. There was always a lot of laughter to be heard when we were together.

After a few years of regular lessons and with a lot of determination, Ian became a very competent jockey. Our dream was to one day buy a house with land so we could keep horses at home. Dogs and other animals also featured on our future wish-list. I had never been particularly maternal and Ian was very happy with the lifestyle we had chosen together, so horses rather than children became our focus and our family.

Chapter 5
A surprise engagement

*"D*ear diary, I've arrived at my hotel in the beautiful Brecon Beacons ready for my client meeting tomorrow. A stream burbles over stones by my window, which is soothing to hear. It's Sunday evening, though, and I'd rather be at home.*

"On my drive down I was thinking about what it was I liked about Ian and why we are so good together after all this time. He's certainly good looking, intelligent, warm and affectionate, but private, respectful and genuine. He's the realist to my idealist, but has imagination, innovation and determination like no-one else I know. He's the considerate to my rash. He makes me think and challenges me – I have to have a bloody good rationale to win any debate. He's helped me achieve stuff I would never have had the confidence to do alone.

"He's not Mr Perfect - he has a stubborn streak like you wouldn't believe, but I wouldn't be sat here writing this if he was faultless because I'd have got bored a long time ago. No, he's not perfect, but he's definitely my Mr Right. I know one thing for sure and that is, Ian is one very special person who I am deeply in love with."

In 1998, eight years after that first kiss and after three years of tyre-wearing journeys up and down the M1 while we established our careers, Ian and I finally moved in together. I'll never forget the first week that Ian joined me to live in the one-bedroom flat I rented close to my work. He was in the process of selling his house in Nottingham so most of his stuff was thankfully still there. I needn't have worried about space though.

He arrived for the weekend and on Monday morning he set off to his new job in Milton Keynes. That afternoon, I arrived home first, excited about welcoming Ian back and spending the evening together. Six o'clock came and went; dinner was cooked; dinner went cold. No sign of Ian. By eight o'clock, I was beside myself with worry.

Neither of us had mobile phones back then so I rang a friend of mine in a total panic.

"What should I do?" I squeaked. "Should I ring hospitals? Should I ring the police to see if there's been an accident?"

She suggested I rang both, but reassured me that he was bound to come home in the next hour or so and was probably being keen on his first day. I rang off, unconvinced. This was not like Ian. The phone immediately rang again, making me jump out of my skin. I grabbed the receiver.

"Hello," I said, as I silently pleaded with the big man upstairs for it not to be the police or a hospital, relaying bad news.

"Hello lovely, it's me. I'm in Milan," said the unmistakable voice of my boyfriend.

"Milan?" I yelled. "What the bleeping hell are you doing in bleeping Milan?"

And this was how it was for the next two years. He was away Monday to Friday, most weeks, travelling all over Europe and to North America, contracted to help corporations safeguard their IT systems from the 'impending' Y2K disaster forecast for the turn of the century which never actually materialised. I wonder if the fact we spent the first few years of our careers living most of the week apart actually contributed to the longevity of our relationship. We were two very independent souls who were madly and deeply in love with each other, but who needed our own space, too.

Despite his weekly absences, we found a rental property in Tring, a small market town in the middle of the scenic chalk uplands that form the Chiltern Hills. This is an area of outstanding beauty and provided the perfect central base for us to live between our offices.

∞ ∞ ∞

In December that same year, we booked a romantic weekend away in Nottingham to celebrate our anniversary of getting together and to revisit our old student haunts. We arrived in the city centre on an overcast and damp Saturday morning, but the bright colourful lights shining out from the shops and their festive spirit twinkling out into the gloom beckoned us into the welcoming warmth within. We strolled along, hand in hand, popping into our favourite shops and remembering our university days and student jaunts.

We turned a corner and the imposing town hall building rose up in front of us, commanding our attention as we crossed the market square. A record store caught my eye.

"Let's go in here," I suggested as I turned towards the open door.

Ian squeezed my hand before letting go. "You go in here. I'm going to nip up the hill to the old town to get something for your Christmas present," he replied, a twinkle in his eye.

We arranged to meet back in the square and 30 minutes later, I saw him heading towards me, wrapped up against the biting wind. I smiled and waved. The sight of him still made my heart leap even after all these years.

Shopping done, we headed to the comfort of our hotel room to spend the rest of the afternoon watching the rugby on TV and relaxing. I sat on the bed, enjoying the thrills and spills of the match while Ian brought our luggage in from the car. Bags unloaded, he settled himself down beside me but seemed on edge.

"You OK?" I asked as he shifted his position yet again.

"Er, can we talk?"

He turned to look at me.

"Uh-oh," I thought. "This sounds serious."

I noticed he had one hand behind his back, which he now moved. I gasped as he held out a beautiful ring: a trio of sparkling diamonds embedded within a platinum band.

"Oh, my God!" I gasped as my hand flew to my open mouth.

"Will you marry me?"

I threw my arms around his neck, laughing and hugging him. It didn't even occur to me until a few minutes later to answer him – something he teased me about afterwards.

For a few minutes, I couldn't speak. My mind whirred like a Catherine wheel as thoughts crackled like sparks around my head and emotions flashed from absolute delight to fear and back again. This was it. A lifelong commitment to one person – marriage – the one thing I had vowed I would never do. Yet, looking at this handsome man in front of me whom I loved with all my heart, with his eyes shining from excitement, I knew, and had perhaps always known from the day we met, that I was meant to be with this person for the rest of my life.

"Well?" he asked, concern creeping over his face as he pulled away to look at me.

"Yes. Yes, of course I will," I exclaimed, shaking from a heady cocktail of anticipation and apprehension.

A much-relieved Ian rummaged around in his suitcase to produce a bottle of champagne he had smuggled in there. The cork popped and we poured the fizzing contents into the hotel room mugs – we knew how to live. That night we went out to celebrate. I felt on top of the world; after all, I was marrying my best friend.

∞ ∞ ∞

"You're getting married in the North – in March?" queried one girlfriend. "Are you completely out of your mind? Actually, don't answer that, I already know you are."

In March 2000, 15 months after our engagement – Ian's business travels prolonged the planning process – we tied the knot in Lancashire. Fate proved the doubters wrong because I awoke the morning of our wedding day with the sun streaming through the curtains. A glorious wintry sunny morning greeted me, the type that makes you feel thankful to be alive.

Hair and make-up done, Mum and I disappeared upstairs, where I changed into my dress, an ivory off-the-shoulder full-length gown with a fitted bodice encrusted with glistening glass beads and a long satin train. It had enough sparkle without being over to the top. As I carefully slid my feet into the matching ivory heels, I felt my inner princess glow as I turned to face my mum.

"Oh sweetheart, you look beautiful."

"I did think about wearing my Doc Martens," I chuckled, as I wiggled one foot, from under the dress, using humour to dissipate my feelings of self-consciousness.

"Kathryn!" Mum rolled her eyes in mock exasperation, before walking over to give me a big hug.

Slowly, carefully, I made my way downstairs to where Dad was waiting in the hallway. He gave a manly cough as I reached him, as if to detract from the emotion he clearly felt. His eyes were watery and his face showed an expression full of pride and love.

"Ready?" he asked.

I nodded and smiled. I felt on top of the world. I can honestly say I didn't have one doubt in my mind that day that marrying Ian was the right path for me.

Ian and I had agreed beforehand that if the day didn't go quite as planned, then we'd accept whatever happened as being part of the occasion. This was fortunate because, as I took the first step down the narrow aisle towards my handsome groom, my upper body lurched forward while one foot remained stationary. My dad was standing on my skirt.

"I'm so sorry," Dad whispered as we limped down the aisle.

"It's OK," I whispered back, while trying to stop the giggles bubbling up inside of me from erupting. "It's not that big a deal."

An hour later, we emerged from the church, man and wife. Pretty crocuses were in full bloom, scattering their pastel-coloured spring cheer like confetti around the village green in front of us.

Our wedding party was just close friends and family; a small and relaxed celebration. The groom's speech, which he was still drafting in the car on the way to the venue, was typically Ian: short, sincere and from the heart.

Unlike the groom's address, my project manager of a husband had meticulously planned and organised our honeymoon. However, he kept our destination a secret from me until we arrived at the airport the morning after our wedding day. I was not going to be disappointed. We flew to the beautiful Italian city of Florence, where we spent a couple of nights before heading off in a hire car to tour the Tuscan countryside and cities. We stayed at the most exquisite hotels in the heart of Pisa, Sienna and, my personal favourite, the 13th-century walled town of San Gimignano.

It was truly romantic and Ian clearly knew the way to his new wife's heart because he had arranged for us to stay for a few days in a farmhouse in the heart of Tuscany, riding horses and eating delicious authentic Italian food. We were the only guests that week so each morning the pair of us would set off for a ride with our guide. Every day we rode for hours, exploring the extensive olive groves and woodland that surrounded our accommodation.

One ride was particularly memorable.

We started out after breakfast. The air was damp and mist swirled around the olive trees, obscuring our view. We ascended a steep wooded hillside, our horses picking their way carefully over tree roots and around the sharp twists and turns as we followed our guide along the narrow tracks. The land eventually levelled out, but we remained within forestation, the leaves dripping cold water down our necks as we ducked to avoid low-lying branches.

After an hour or so in the saddle, we arrived at a clearing where we found a small wooden hut. Smoke was streaming vertically out of the chimney and the glow of a lit stove flickered through the window, drawing us closer to its homely comforts.

We dismounted and tied our horses up by looping their reins over a tree branch just outside the door. As we entered this rustic cabin, the smell of toasting bruschetta seeped into my nostrils and my stomach responded with an audible rumble. Stood by the oven was Pietro, the white-haired cook from the farmhouse. He was busy preparing our delicious brunch. As bright orange sparks flew up from the fire, golden fizzing liquor – Prosecco – was poured into two glasses to celebrate our arrival. I shivered as the cool bubbles slipped down my throat. I hadn't realised just how soggy and cold I had become, riding out in the constant drizzle. I moved closer to the fire to get maximum benefit from the heat. Ian joined me, clinking his glass against mine, a huge grin of delight on his face. This was my idea of heaven: horses, stunning scenery, delicious food, sparkling wine and my gorgeous husband. What wasn't there to love?

Horses and the countryside were our shared interests, and what joy they brought.

Chapter 6
Equestrian dreams fulfilled

A few months into married life and our family expanded to three. We were now both in full-time employment and settled in our home so we felt it was the right time for us to look for our own horse.

We didn't have to wait long before Willow, a pretty middleweight mare, joined our clan. She was a bay, her coat being the colour of mahogany with a black mane and tail. A small white circle of hair, the size of a 50p piece, sat in the middle of her forehead and another flash of white ran vertically between her nostrils.

Ian's mum came with us when we went to see her for the first time.

"Oh, look at that trot," exclaimed Pat in awe as Willow trotted towards both of us with Ian by her side.

She had a very relaxed swinging stride, which would award us high marks in dressage in months to come. And her hooves! They were the size of soup plates. But, my goodness, we never had any problems with her feet or limbs.

We checked her over for any unusual lumps and bumps that might indicate underlying issues or previous injuries.

"Kathryn, Ian, come and look at this."

Pat stood by Willow's head, her index finger stroking a specific point on Willow's chest.

"She has a prophet's thumbprint, look."

Sure enough, there under Pat's finger was a shallow indentation in the mare's skin where your thumb could comfortably sit. Legend has it that after days of wandering in the desert, the Prophet Mohammed sent his herd of thirsty horses to a nearby oasis to drink. Those that came back to him, when called, he marked with his thumbprint as a sign of their loyalty. It's thought to signify a special horse, a descendent of these original broodmares.

If she had been human, Willow would have been the matronly type – your dependable best friend – and I adored her. Mares can be tricky to handle given they have all their hormones intact so they can be prone to mood swings. They are, after all, the female equivalent of a stallion and you always handle the latter with care. In equestrian circles, we say "You ask a mare, tell a gelding and negotiate with a stallion." We were, however, very lucky with Willow. She was a sweet-natured, honest horse who tried her heart out for us. If I'd had a difficult day at work, I'd go and see my friend Willow and share my troubles with her. She would munch on her hay with a thoughtful expression on her face and sometimes nudge me with her nose, just to let me know she was listening.

I felt as if she was saying "You'll be OK, honey. You're doing a great job. Now, don't fret, and give me a hug."

She was a girl's girl and over the years I formed a very special bond with her.

However, she was only six years old when we bought her so hadn't been in training for very long. Given our lack of experience of horse ownership, bringing on a youngster wasn't perhaps the wisest choice though, having owned several animals now, I firmly believe that they choose you rather than the other way round. This was certainly the case with Willow. We may have faced a few difficulties at the beginning due to our inexperience, but she taught us a lot and we were keen to learn.

With the help of knowledgeable trainers, Willow developed into a super horse who achieved far more than we ever imagined possible during those early days. Furthermore, our experiences with Willow stood us in good stead for when we attained another family member, a year later, during a riding holiday in Ireland.

We travelled to the west coast, where we stayed in Loughrea, a small market town close to the city of Galway. Each morning we travelled to the riding establishment based a few miles outside the town. Some days we would saddle up and head off around the many off-road trails in the area; on others, we would congregate at the local cross-country course and enjoy fast and exhilarating rides over the fences there.

The undulating green fields of the Galway countryside provided a fantastic terrain for cobweb cleansing gallops. Dry limestone walls divided the landscape, providing natural obstacles for us to jump. Cars were few and far between on the country lanes. Bridleways were in abundance, leading us into pockets of woodland where we could shelter from the inevitable rain of the Emerald Isle. It was horse riding paradise.

On arriving at the cross-country course, we'd scramble into our instructor Will's battered Land Rover and rattle our way over the rough ground towards a herd of Connemara horses, usually huddled together under a tree against the elements. This hardy breed, native to the west coast of Ireland, has compact bodies and strong short limbs, so excel at jumping. Will would select a couple for us to ride and we'd hop out of the vehicle to catch our chosen steeds for the next riding session. Our mounts were often young, but by golly they could jump.

Ian was in his element here, much more than I was. I enjoyed riding along the trails, but when it came to the jumping I wasn't so brave. My lack of confidence meant that I approached the fences far too fast – and often with my eyes closed – in the belief that this would get me to the other side. Will wasn't impressed by my seemingly reckless tactics.

"You'll break yer bloody neck if yer ride like that," he shouted.

To illustrate his point, he walked his horse towards the fence – an imposing hedge – and over they popped. He grinned and winked as he turned back to me.

Will was no spring chicken and walking looked a struggle, but astride a horse he was magical to watch.

I sighed. To be honest, I much preferred training the horses in the arena than out here in the open fields. Ian, on the other hand, loved every minute and was always the first to volunteer when Will came over to where we were having lunch and asked who was up for a second ride. Some afternoons I opted to sit inside with another hot whisky, if I wasn't feeling particularly bold, or I rode one of the horses in the sandy enclosure adjacent to the stable barn.

At the end of a long day in the saddle, Ian and I would return to the homely comforts of O'Dea's, a hotel in the middle of Loughrea town. The entrance off the carpark took us down a freezing cold corridor, past the nightclub, to the main bar, where we would peel off our damp coats and tug off our muddy boots. They were taken down to the boiler room to dry off, ready for the next day. After a hot bath, we'd head back to the bar to sit in front of the open fire and sip on a pint of cold Guinness before going out for supper to one of the local restaurants with the other riders in our group. Here we spent many an evening sharing stories about our lives and riding adventures. All came to this relaxed and informal setting to enjoy the countryside on horseback.

Unbeknownst to me, during our first visit to Loughrea Ian was eyeing up a large gelding called Sligo Bells. He was a beautiful looking boy. His golden chestnut coat was the colour of autumn bracken and a wide white blaze ran the length of his face. His mane and tail were lighter in colour, highlighted by gingery flecks of gold that many a woman would pay a fortune to have in her own hair.

At five years old, he already stood at 17.2 hh and looked enormous to me. His training was fairly basic in terms of dressage, but like all the horses in Will's yard he had a fantastic jump with huge scope. Will told us that, as the Master of Foxhounds for the Galway Blazers, he often took Sligo Bells out for a day's hunting.

Sensing a deal was in the offing, Will allowed us to ride out, alone – Ian on Sligo Bells and me on a relatively small 15 hh sprightly horse, aptly named Sligo Bay, whom I had enjoyed jumping the day before. We had a super ride out around the local woodland and, on returning to the yard, jumped over some fences in the field alongside the stables. Ian loved Sligo Bells and I fell for his gentle nature.

"I think we should buy him," Ian said.

"I agree," I replied. "It will be lovely to ride out together."

"Shall we go and speak to Will about price?" Ian's eyes were shining with excitement.

I nodded, and before too long hands were shaken. A deal was struck. Sligo Bells was ours providing the vet considered him fit and well.

We travelled back to Ireland for the vet inspection a couple of weeks later, where Sligo Bells passed with flying colours.

Another three weeks and he made the long journey over to England by ferry. On the day he was due, I received a phone call.

"Hi there, I'm transporting your horse. I have an address, but can you give me some extra directions?"

"Sure," I replied, and gave the driver some landmarks to help him locate our stables, situated down quite a narrow lane.

"I'll meet you at the end of the road and then you can follow me to the yard."

Well, I was in for a shock. There I was, parked at the end of the lane, waiting to see the horsebox making its way down the hill towards me. But this was no ordinary horsebox. This was a giant articulated lorry capable of carrying about eight horses. I still don't know how it squeezed down the lane or how the driver skilfully reversed up the curved driveway to deposit our new horse.

The ramp lowered and Sligo Bells emerged, looking tired and thin after his epic journey over the Irish Sea. I heard a collective intake of breath and much sucking of teeth by our stable mates as we led him to the stable barn. They clearly thought we had lost the plot somewhere in the Galway countryside and I was beginning to wonder if they were right. He was green, having received very little training other than jumping, so Team White, as we now called ourselves, faced another steep learning curve.

We settled our new arrival in an isolation stable away from the other horses to prevent the spread of any infection. His stall was adjacent to the barn entrance and each time we opened the door, his pink velvety nose would appear through the crack, eager to say hello.

We renamed our new friend Moose – The Irish Moose, to give him his full competition name. At that time, top British event rider Ian Stark rode a huge bay horse called The Moose. Given we planned to do some cross-country riding ourselves, we thought this was the perfect name for our gangly Irish youngster.

Another year on, and Ian and I were thoroughly enjoying our lives as horse owners. Every evening was taken up either riding or caring for Moose and Willow, while the weekends were spent travelling to compete at jumping and dressage events. We were the ultimate equestrian enthusiasts. I often pinched myself in disbelief of how fortunate I was, living the life I had dreamed of as a child with the added bonus of having a partner who was as enthusiastic as me.

Moose was the maverick – the naughty schoolboy – while Willow was the class swot. Funny how animals reflect their owners' traits. The pair got on very well, though I think the affection was a little one-sided. Willow would always whinny for Moose if they were separated, but the call was never reciprocated.

I recall one afternoon at the stables when John greeted us with a stern look on his face.

"Your mare gave us a scare today," he started, his features crinkling as a smile broke through the serious façade.

"Is she OK?" I asked, wondering what on earth had been going on.

"Oh yes, she's fine," he continued. "She managed to undo the latch on her stable door and wandered off to her field. We found her happily grazing. Very sneaky!"

I laughed.

I imagined her ample backside disappearing from view while Moose, looking on from his stable, would have been saying "Hey, what about me? You're going to be in so much trouble, Willow, when they find you gone."

The autumn months brought their own entertainment, like watching Ian and Moose sauntering along the hedge that bordered the arena where we trained. Moose gave Ian the perfect platform from which to pick and eat the deliciously plump blackberries that were out of reach of anyone on foot. Moose, thankful not to be schooling, would obediently walk slowly, blissfully unaware of the scrumping going on above.

Ian was well and truly bitten by the cross-country riding bug so I decided to book a weekend away at Burghley International Horse Trials for his birthday. This event is held each September in the glorious grounds of Burghley House, Stamford. Riders arrive from all over the world to compete and the event is televised.

It was 2003, the year that top British rider Pippa Funnell and eventing royalty Zara Phillips battled it out for first place, with Pippa in contention to become Rolex Grand Slam Champion if she won this, her third four-star event of the year. Expectations were high for a thrilling event and we weren't disappointed.

Before the competition started, we joined a group of other spectators on a course walk with Team GB stalwart, Jeanette Breakwell. The sun was beaming down on us as we followed Jeanette around the cross-country course, our little group oohing and ahhing at the enormous fences that these brilliant riders and horses have to jump. Until you see them close up, you really don't appreciate their size. Towards the end, we approached the infamous Cottesmore Leap – a yawning ditch, large enough to accommodate a Land Rover jeep, in front of an equally imposing brush fence. This wide trench helps the horses see their take-off point so, in essence, it's a horse-friendly fence. However, that enormous ditch makes this sort of obstacle a real rider frightener – so much so that Jeanette wouldn't walk up to the edge of it, preferring to stay some distance away.

"If I go any closer, I'll never have the confidence to jump it," she explained.

The riders walk the course several times to familiarise themselves with every twist and turn and lump and bump in the terrain so they are fully prepared when they're galloping at great speed over the jumps.

Ian was inspired by the walk.

"I think we should event Moose and Willow."

Chapter 7
Eventing glory

Ian never did anything by halves so it didn't surprise me when, the following year, we became members of the sport's affiliated organisation, British Eventing, and training began in earnest for our first competition.

The eventing season starts in March and runs throughout the summer months to October. Most weekends we were travelling around the UK to compete, often within glorious country estates which are otherwise closed to the public. They are all-day affairs – known as one-day events – during which you compete in three riding disciplines: dressage, show jumping and then the thrilling final phase, the cross-country, when you gallop over a course of solid obstacles.

The partnership you build with your horses as you train and compete in this sport is incredible. They have to place their trust in you to steer them over the jumps, while you have to put your trust in their athletic ability as mistakes can be very costly to horse and rider.

One-day events are the mainstay of the eventing world and are where all the top riders compete to qualify their horses for the major three-day events like Badminton and Burghley. It meant that we frequently competed alongside our eventing heroes, like Pippa Funnell, William Fox-Pitt and Zara Phillips. It was such a thrill, especially as most of these professional riders were more than happy, when asked, to give advice to those of us who are amateurs and part-timers in the sport.

I think it's fair to say that it didn't take long for eventing to become a major part of our life. And, when we weren't at the stables, we were watching old footage of the big three-day international events to pick up tips from the pros.

On a Friday evening before a competition, we'd hurry up to the stables after work, eager to pack the horsebox, plait the horses' manes and clean our tack ready for an early departure the next morning. The alarm would ring out, often before sunrise. We'd sleepily pull on jogging bottoms and sweatshirts over our competition clothing before heading to the yard where our beautiful horses greeted us with a welcoming whicker. Detecting our excitement, they would bound up the lorry ramp, eager to get started.

Driving into a field, with the dew still glistening on the grass and the sense of anticipation hanging in the air, was very special. Even thinking about it now, I can feel my stomach flutter with excitement and nerves. Horses whinnied and stamped on the lorries, while riders or their grooms scurried around, preparing water buckets and various pieces of equipment for the day ahead. Before too long, the cross-country tannoy would crackle into life and the commentary would begin, adding to the atmosphere.

Leaving Moose and Willow to munch on their hay nets in the horsebox, Ian and I would pick up our competitor numbers from the secretary's tent before seeking out the coffee stand. Grabbing cups of steaming caffeine-rich nectar, we'd walk the cross-country and show jumping courses to familiarise ourselves with the challenges that lay ahead. We'd then return to the lorry to saddle up, ready to warm up for the dressage.

Being out in the fresh air amongst like-minded people fed my soul. I felt content and a sense of belonging at these events.

The camaraderie between competitors was wonderful – we never felt as if we were competing against anyone. It's really a test of the horse and rider combination against the jumping tracks. Because it's such a dangerous sport, even the most expert riders end up eating dirt on a fairly regular basis, especially when training their young horses. So everyone is very down to earth, including the top riders, who will stop and chat or answer questions. I was rather chuffed when Andrew Nicholson, a well-known professional rider from New Zealand, complimented me on the system I'd set up to fill our water buckets.

The plastic square water containers we took with us to shows were too heavy for me to lift when full so I'd tip one of them carefully onto its side, balancing it partway out of the groom's door in the side of our horsebox. I'd then place a bucket on top of the stepladders we had, such that I could open the tap on the container and let the contents pour out. Nothing particularly ingenious, but it worked.

"Neat system you got there," Andrew remarked as he strode past me.

Feeling a little star struck, my cheeks flushed red as I stuttered a thank you and then had to close the tap quickly before the contents of the bucket spilled over into my boots.

Ian's finest hour was at Gatcombe Park horse trials in the novice level class. At this venue, the show jumping and cross-country jumps were always fair but up to height so it took a plucky horse and jockey to get round both. None other than the Princess Royal, still a keen competitor herself, designs the cross-country course, which is a bold galloping track that suited the long-striding Moose.

On this particular day, Moose was more relaxed than usual and as such, he showed off his moves in the dressage arena to post his best score of the season.

Normally, his ears would visibly droop when he saw the white boards marking out the arena – dressage was a necessary evil to get through before the thrill of jumping. The good fortune continued in the show jumping. With a few events at this level under their belts, Moose and Ian entered this phase with more confidence and finesse. They left all the poles up, so headed to the cross-country on a decent score.

Down at the start line, Moose was clearly happy at the prospect of galloping over the old Gloucestershire turf because he leapt out of the start box and set off at a "hell of a lick", according to the commentator.

The commentators are an essential part of the competition because they track the riders' progress. The fence judges – all volunteers – communicate with the commentary team via radios and are essential for improving the safety of this sport. If a horse or rider has a fall at their fence, they report back to the commentary team, who will then organise on-site paramedics to attend if needed.

"Ian White and The Irish Moose clear fence 15 in fine style," reported the commentator, his voice booming over the countryside.

I smiled as I stood by the water jump awaiting their arrival. I didn't have to wait long as Ian came into view from another field. Moose's ears were pricked and I could hear Ian giving him vocal encouragement and instructions as they approached the water:

"Steady; whoa there; good boy."

Ian moved his shoulders back to sit more upright in the saddle in order to help Moose rebalance as they entered the water via a slightly sloping gravel bank. The pair jumped up a step onto a platform and a couple of strides later splashed back into the water before exiting and galloping onto the next fence, away in the distance. I overheard an elderly gentleman, sitting beside me on his shooting stick, say approvingly to his friend,

"Textbook stuff. Now that's how you jump through water."

I smiled, feeling very proud of my boys, and hurried back to the finish line to greet them.

"Woohoo!" I shouted as they completed.

Ian enthusiastically patted Moose's neck, which glistened with sweat, veins standing proud due to his exertion.

They had made it round with just five time penalties to add to their score so finished in 10th place with a double clear, a result that was testament to Ian's hard work and dedication. For all three phases to go well is no mean feat, which is why finishing in the top 10 is a great achievement.

The icing on the cake came later that day, when Ian attended the prize-giving where he was presented his rosette by none other than Princess Anne with me, my parents and Ian's parents proudly looking on. What a glorious day for Team White.

These one-day events were family affairs, with Ian's mum and dad being our biggest supporters. Their presence made these events even more special for us. Pat, who was thrilled to bits that her son and daughter-in-law were eventers, became chief picnic-ateer. She'd pack a hearty lunch of homemade sausage rolls, sandwiches and crisps plus carrots for the horses, of course. And, after all the excitement of the day, she'd produce a large thermos flask of hot black coffee accompanied by a delicious slab of home-baked cake – sticky oaty flapjack for Ian and a gooey chocolate brownie for me. Ian's dad was our video-cameraman and photographer so we have a lot of our eventing adventures captured for posterity.

And, of course, Ian and I supported each other. Ian was the risk taker in our partnership so he thought nothing of entering events at higher levels and pushing himself out of his own comfort zone. Meanwhile, I wasn't going to be left behind so, with Ian's encouragement and thanks to my competitive streak, I achieved far more than I ever dreamed possible.

This included the completion of my first novice level event, where top Australian eventer Bill Levett kindly accompanied me down to the cross-country start line. The fences were at least a metre in height and seemed enormous, even though we had jumped fences of that size in training. I was so nervous, especially given that Willow had slipped in the show jumping and consequently had a fence down. Bill, whom I had met through a mutual contact and whom we had had lessons with, chatted to me the whole way there and, despite having his own preparation to do, made sure I was OK warming up.

"You'll be fine," Bill reassured me as the steward called me over to the start box.

"Ten seconds to go," she announced.

I took a deep breath and steered Willow into the three-sided enclosure ready to be counted down.

"3-2-1 – Go! Good luck," called the starter as Willow and I emerged onto the cross-country course.

I focused on the first fence ahead of us – a simple and inviting roll-top well within our capabilities. Willow sailed over it and I patted her neck as we cantered on to the next obstacle, with Bill's words of advice ringing in my ears. We successfully negotiated each of the 23 jumps, including ditches, steps and water. Hurtling towards the finish line, I could see Ian and his parents cheering us on. I had a huge grin on my face as Willow and I completed the course and I will be forever grateful to Bill for his thoughtfulness that day.

The more we competed, the more our confidence grew as our skills improved. Rather than feeling sick with nerves at the cross-country start, I began to relax and really enjoy this phase. A few of the officials also recognised us as we returned to some of our favourite venues and would often strike up conversation while we waited to enter the start enclosure, which made us feel more at home.

At one event, Willow had scored highly in the dressage and jumped clear round the show jumping. Having walked the cross-country course, I knew it was well within our capabilities so I was in high spirits as I rode down to the start.

"Have you had a successful day so far?" asked the steward, before inquiring after Willow's breeding, which I relayed briefly while entering the start box.

"Ten seconds," he interjected, before adding, "She has a fine backside."

This was the last comment I heard before the countdown began. I assumed he was talking about Willow, but given my good mood that day, I couldn't resist giving a little wiggle of my own derrière as we surged forwards and galloped on to the first fence. We completed in fine style and our efforts were rewarded with a second place.

Chapter 8
Practice makes perfect

Although we were classed as amateurs because we didn't make a living from horses, we took our sport seriously and practised hard. Horse riding has its dangers at the best of times, given the unpredictable behaviour of these amazing animals, but add the element of jumping solid fences at speed and you significantly increase the risk of serious injury or even fatality.

Developing our skills to minimise injuries to ourselves and our horses was paramount. Therefore, we dedicated a lot of our time to training.

As a former professional showjumper, our friend John was the perfect coach for this phase, especially as we were based with him. He was also very fond of Moose and loved to test this horse's ability. Moose had an impressive leap, leaving a lot of air between him and the jump below – so much so that at one event, Ian had to duck quickly to prevent being plucked from the saddle when negotiating a cross-country fence with a canopy.

"Let's see how high this boy can jump," announced John during one lesson, when he kept increasing the height of the fences each time Ian successfully completed the course.

Eventually the last jump was the same height as the wings, the vertical supports at each end of the coloured poles.

"Hold on tight, Ian!" I called from the corner of the arena where Willow and I stood awaiting our turn.

Ian wasn't going to miss this opportunity to fly. They approached the final obstacle. Moose's ears were pricked, focused on the target ahead. Ian's face was serious with concentration. Over they sailed, Ian barely visible above Moose's head as he crouched low in the saddle. His delight lit up the entire school when they landed, leaving the poles safely in their cups.

Now it was my and Willow's turn.

"You are going to put those down for us, aren't you?" I asked with some trepidation.

"Don't you worry," John replied. "You concentrate on getting that mare of yours into a nice energetic canter."

With the fences lowered, I circled Willow at one end of the arena, ready to point her at the first jump.

"Ding, ding," shouted Ian, imitating the bell that usually signals the start of a jumping round in competition.

Round we went, Willow elegantly clearing each fence. We turned the final corner and approached the last obstacle. Though much lower than it had been for Ian, the poles still looked a long way from the ground, so I kicked Willow on, worried we might lose impulsion.

"Bloody eventers!" yelled John as we cleared it in fine style and hurtled towards the end of the course.

I patted Willow's neck. "Thanks John, I'll take that as a compliment."

Hill work was another key part of our fitness training and the Chiltern Hills in which we lived lent themselves perfectly to this. John let us use one of his fields for such a purpose so Ian and I would walk the horses down to the bottom, count to three, turn round and up we'd blast. Well, that was the theory.

"On your marks – go," I'd shout while turning Willow to face the incline. "Come on girl, let's beat the boys."

On paper, Moose, with his long legs and streamlined part-thoroughbred body, was always going to be faster than my beautiful middleweight mare, who tried her heart out for me to gallop up that incline. However, Moose struggled to contain his excitement so as Willow and I left the starting blocks, I'd look round to see Ian still at the bottom on a Moose who was bouncing around on the spot.

"What the heck are you doing, mate?" Ian would cry out as he tried to get Moose to focus.

Then I'd hear the familiar pounding of hooves as the boys finally got their act together and started to gain on us, with Moose putting in the odd defiant buck here and there. Unfortunately for them, they'd usually given us such a head start that Willow and I were victorious more times than not.

However, the boys had the last laugh during cross-country training. All was going very well and as we approached the final jump, a water complex that we had both jumped before, I was feeling rather confident. Having watched Ian and Moose clear the easier option, I decided to push my luck and opt for the more advanced way in, via a larger fence, followed by a bounce off the step into the water. Unluckily, Willow missed her footing on the step.

Splash!

She fell sideways into the water – a few feet deep – fully submerging the pair of us. It felt like minutes, but a few seconds later we both surfaced, me spluttering and coughing while desperately trying to free one foot from the stirrup. I untangled myself from Willow as she scrambled to her feet, shaking moisture from her ears and then from the rest of her body. As we got ourselves sorted, the sound of hysterical laughter wafted over from the bank from where Ian and Moose stood watching.

I glowered at them both, unamused, but the sound of my boots squelching as I led Willow out of the pond did nothing to settle Mr White's mirth. Let me tell you, it was most unpleasant cantering home, the cold air intensified by the wet clothing clinging to my body. My feet swam around in the puddles in my boots. I shudder just remembering it. I salute all those amazing competitors who have fallen into the infamous lake at Badminton and still jump around the rest of that enormous course. Trying to stay on board a very slippery saddle is no mean feat.

Chapter 9
Team White diaries

It was through our involvement in the world of eventing that I realised my passion for writing. In 2004, the same year we started competing in the sport, an online eventing magazine launched. Aimed at amateur riders like Ian and me, the website featured rider interviews and event reports from around the country as well as lots of useful advice.

Having experienced a few difficulties downloading an instructional video, part of a feature they were running, I contacted the site owner and editor, Janie, to see if she could help. This initial correspondence led to regular email exchanges as we 'connected' through our mutual love of eventing and horses to share our experiences.

The emails showcased my writing style, which Janie liked, so she invited me to write a monthly column describing my and Ian's eventing exploits. What a thrill and an honour to become an integral part of this online eventing community. Much to my surprise, the 'Team White' column proved popular and we gained a following – so much so, our lovely readers would come over at events to say hello and meet Moose and Willow, the real stars of Team White.

I loved writing this column and would pass each draft on to Ian to check and edit. He was great at making sure the information was relevant and checking that the story flowed. Ian wasn't one to throw compliments out without good justification so I always felt particularly pleased whenever he thought an article of mine was well written.

The magazine grew in popularity and so did my confidence as a writer. I wrote a few articles based on my own ideas as well as reporting from the one-day events where Ian and I were competing. I was living the dream. Here I was, fully immersed in the sport, not only as a competitor but also as an equestrian journalist, meeting and interviewing many of my heroes from the sport, including riders, trainers and officials. A highlight was spending time with British eventer Pippa Funnell, alongside more experienced and eminent journalists from the equestrian and popular press, when she held an open day at her yard. She was celebrating her incredible Rolex Grand Slam win, when she won four consecutive four-star events within a 12-month period.

I totally lose track of time when I write, so absorbed am I in the task. Seeing your name in print is such a thrill, though at the time of submission I feel nervous, because you expose a little bit of your soul in every piece you create and you pray for positive feedback. Writing for the magazine was a reward in itself, but, in addition, Janie generously provided us with clothing and saddle cloths, all emblazoned with the magazine's logo, and organised training days with highly respected instructors. Ian and I felt like professionals and loved every minute of our association with Janie and her team. These were halcyon days and the exposure led to writing opportunities with *Eventing Magazine*, the *Eventing Horse Owners Association* and other equestrian brands.

A high point that Ian and I shared came in September 2007, when we reported from the international three-day event held every year on the Blenheim Palace estate in Oxfordshire. I had already spent time with Janie in the press tent at Badminton in May the same year, where, much to my excitement, we interviewed riders alongside TV's Clare Balding. So I had some idea of what to expect, but, at Blenheim, she entrusted Ian and me to report without her as chaperone. What an honour.

We were in our element, especially when members of the British team selected for the forthcoming European Eventing Championships held a press conference before heading off to compete in Pratoni, Italy.

Ian nudged me as he sat beside me in the press marquee. "Can you believe we're actually doing this?" he asked excitedly.

This was our world – our shared passion. Sadly, this was to be the last eventing competition we would attend as reporters or riders.

Chapter 10
A sign of things to come?

Octctober 2007, and after giving the horses a well-deserved month off, we began preparing for the following season. During the winter, we competed in dressage and showjumping competitions to fine-tune our skills and maintain the horses' fitness levels.

One weekend we went to a dressage competition where Ian rode Willow because she had a flair for this phase, unlike Moose, and he wanted to fine-tune his test riding.

A dressage test comprises a sequence of movements ridden at specific markers placed around the arena. There are a series of these tests at each competency level, so you pre-learn the test being judged on the day, execute the movements in the correct sequence and then receive the judge's comments and a mark out of 10 for each movement. The winner is the rider who receives the highest overall percentage mark.

That day, somewhere in his test, Ian went wrong. I watched from the sidelines with a couple of friends, who were also competing in the same class, so they were familiar with the test being ridden.

"He should have trotted at B," remarked Neil, looking at his own test sheet to double-check. "He should have turned up the arena there," he continued.

Normally, the judge will ring a bell if you make an error so you then have to stop and restart the test at the point of your first mistake. However, this judge seemed as oblivious to any inaccuracy as the rider. The bell wasn't rung and Ian continued.

The one thing that all tests have in common is they finish with a trot or canter down the centre of the arena towards the judge, with a halt at a pre-designated point. The rider salutes the judge by dropping one hand to their side to acknowledge the end. To this day, I don't know how Ian did this, but despite his slip-up he managed to end the test correctly, trotting in the right direction towards the judge before halting and saluting. I couldn't understand how he had gone wrong and realised from talking to him after the test that he hadn't even been aware of his mistake.

Remarkably, Ian wasn't penalised so he and Willow came fifth.

Looking back, I wonder if this was the first sign that something wasn't right with Ian, though on reading some of my diary entries from the second half of that year, I was surprised to see that we had quite a few disagreements, something I had clearly forgotten. And I do recall coming back from one event when we were both tired. I can't remember what I said to Ian, but I think I reminded him to do something and he mocked me, something he had never done before.

I put it all down to us both being in demanding jobs with the added commitment of the horses and thought nothing more about it.

Part Two

A Tragic Twist

Chapter 11
The hell begins

"5, 4, 3, 2, 1!" shouted the DJ excitedly as he encouraged the New Year's revellers in our local pub to count down to the start of 2008. The pub stood a few yards from our home and I groaned with frustration at the ongoing noise. I turned once more under the duvet, trying to find a more comfortable position. I hadn't slept at all well, despite coming to bed early, and I longed to drop off into a deep slumber.

Ian was sleeping upstairs in the attic bedroom. He had been feeling more tired than normal for the past few weeks. Despite his daytime lethargy, he could not settle at night and, consequently, neither of us was getting the sleep we needed to cope with our busy lives. We decided the only way to resolve this for the short term was to sleep in separate rooms.

I buried my head under my pillow, using my hands to press the soft feather-filled material around my ears, to try and muffle the beginnings of *Auld Lang Syne* which now floated across the road. I loathe New Year. It's a night filled with so much expectation, which it rarely lives up to in my experience. This New Year's Eve there was something else keeping me awake, something needling away at the back of my mind, in the mists of my subconscious, but I couldn't pinpoint what it was. I just had a sense of foreboding.

That nagging doubt arose again a week later, when Ian flew to Ireland on business for a couple of days, a trip he had done several times before. On his way back from the airport, he rang me from the car as he negotiated his way round the M25 motorway. It was a route he was familiar with, but that night he missed his exit junction, twice.

"I feel so sleepy," he complained to me. "I can't believe I've just driven past again. Sorry, my lovely, but I'll be a bit late."

He eventually arrived home frustrated with himself as well as feeling exhausted. He was also finding concentrating at work difficult.

"I feel like I'm zoning out of meetings and then jolting back to consciousness partway through a discussion," he explained.

This was uncharacteristic of someone as conscientious as he was, but we attributed this lack of concentration to his hectic schedule.

However, at the end of the month, there was no improvement.

At a family gathering to celebrate his dad's birthday, everyone was on good form, including our young nieces and nephews, who kept us entertained with football in the garden and the offer of crayoning and playing board games. Everyone, that is, except Uncle Ian, who snoozed in one of the armchairs, having almost fallen asleep at the lunch table. This was not normal. Usually he was the first to volunteer to play games with the children while the rest of us sat around chatting.

My brother-in-law flashed me a concerned look as snoring emanated from the comfy chair in the corner of the conservatory.

"Is he OK? He doesn't look it," he whispered to me.

I looked over to where Ian was, and that unsettled feeling in the back of my mind returned. I shook my head.

"He's fine," I lied. "He's having a busy time at work."

Nevertheless, I insisted I drove home that evening.

"Ian, I think you should see your doctor," I tentatively suggested as we sat in the car.

I looked across at my husband, who wasn't all that alert despite his afternoon nap.

"OK," he responded, followed by a large yawn.

This was most unusual given Ian's general reluctance to go near a doctor. I pushed my luck a bit further.

"Actually, I don't think you should risk driving this week until we get to the bottom of your tiredness," I finished.

Once again, he agreed. Something definitely wasn't right.

Ian and I worked for the same company at the time. I was an employee, working in clinical research. Ian was a freelance consultant working for the manufacturing division. It meant we could work from the same location so I drove us in each day and he used a spare desk in our open-plan office.

On the Friday, Ian and I arranged to meet for lunch to celebrate the end of the week. At the agreed time, I went over to reception so we could walk to the staff canteen together, but there was no sign of the ever-punctual Ian. I waited and waited. He didn't show up. This was not like my husband at all. Where was he? I went back into the main office area and there he was, holding onto the edge of some cupboards close to his desk, his face as white as the shirt on his back.

"Are you OK?" I asked.

He shook his head and explained how, on his way to meet me, he had suddenly felt light-headed. By grasping the cupboards, he had avoided collapsing to the floor. Although he had steadied himself, he hadn't felt confident about walking any further.

Lunch was abandoned, and I rang our doctor's surgery to book him in for that afternoon. He was given a once-over and blood samples were taken.

"I'll be in touch once we get the results."

And that was it. There was nothing more we could do but wait.

Later, that same evening, I awoke with a start. Ian and I were back sleeping in the same bed and I was aware of someone moving around the bedroom and whimpering.

"Ian?" I called out into the darkness.

I heard an anguished groan as I switched on the light.

"My head really hurts," he moaned, holding his forehead with one hand, a pained expression on his face.

The bright light was clearly not helping and he was almost in tears with the intensity of pain.

"I'm calling the doctor," I said, scrambling out of bed.

"No, no!" exclaimed Ian. "I'll be alright. I just need to get some paracetamol."

Now, Ian was no drama queen. During the 18 years we had been together, my husband had only ever been off work due to illness for two days, one of which had been self-inflicted with alcohol while the other was on his return from a business trip to India. He was clearly in agony. I reached for the phone to ring the NHS helpline.

"On a scale of 1 to 10, how bad is your pain?"

I relayed the questions from the nurse on the other end of the telephone.

Still gripping his head in anguish, Ian whispered, "10, oh God, 10."

He needed to be examined urgently, and the nurse agreed.

Satisfied that meningitis could be eliminated, she advised us to go to the local accident and emergency department – "just to be on the safe side," she reassured us.

I helped my husband get dressed and gently steered him out to the car. During our journey to the hospital, I pulled over twice to let him get out and vomit. My stomach churned over and over with concern as I heard my darling man retching by the side of the road in the blackness. By the time we arrived at the hospital, 20 minutes later, he could barely walk. Once more I supported him as we carefully made our way towards the reception desk.

Our dramatic entrance warranted a quick response from the hospital medical team, who swiftly admitted Ian. Based on a physical examination, the doctor diagnosed a severe migraine and administered painkillers and an anti-sickness tablet. After about an hour, Ian felt better and was discharged. We were both relieved that the doctors suspected nothing more serious so didn't think to push for any further tests or scans.

The headaches didn't go away, but the blood tests came back negative so Ian took pain relief tablets as needed, and continued working.

"Contractors have to be on their knees before they give up paid work," was his mantra.

Thankfully, his role allowed for home working.

We returned to see the doctor a couple more times, who couldn't offer any further clues as to the cause of the headaches so just dispensed ever stronger medication.

I researched Ian's symptoms online for possible causes. I felt sure he had a virus or the symptoms were stress-related, given his recent workload. I dismissed a lot of other possible, albeit uncommon, ailments. I emailed my thoughts to my manager, who was a medic. I had already spoken to him about Ian's tiredness, asking if he could give any guidance, and he too thought it was probably a virus that would resolve with rest. However, our recent hospital trip and the fact the headaches weren't easing clearly sparked something in Dan's mind because this time he emailed me back.

"RING THE DOCTOR AND INSIST ON SCANS."

Despite the capitalisation, I still didn't feel Ian's illness was anything to panic about; after all, cancer and other life-threatening illnesses happened to other people.

Meanwhile, Ian was spending an increasing amount of time in bed, trying to escape his throbbing painful head. I didn't want to disturb his sleep so, having received Dan's response, I drove to our doctor's surgery alone to organise another appointment. This time, I planned to accompany Ian and request the necessary scans. Ian was very good at putting on a brave face and I felt sure he was giving the impression he was yet another burnt-out businessman.

I entered the reception area and straightened my back, trying to walk a bit taller to make me look stronger than I felt inside. I hated conflict and normally avoided confrontations at all costs. I knew that requesting an appointment for that day at an already overstretched surgery was not going to be a walk in the park.

I swear the receptionist could smell my fear. But, I thought of Ian lying at home, suffering. I pushed my shoulders back in defiance. I had to stand my ground and be resilient. Taking a deep breath, I fixed her with my best steely stare and repeated my request more forcefully.

"And I'm not moving from here until you book him in," I added, managing to keep my voice from wavering.

Thankfully, she relented.

"Come with me," she instructed, having tapped something into her computer. She accompanied me to a small room next to the waiting area where there was a phone. "Wait here and one of the doctors will ring you on this."

And off she went, back to her desk.

I stood there, feeling very small and alone. All the bravado I had mustered for my entrance melted away. Despair filled my body and I held onto the small table in front of me for support. My husband was obviously very sick, with no solution in sight, yet the doctors didn't seem to be in any great rush to help us.

The phone sprang into life and I grabbed the hand-piece.

"Hello, I'm Dr Johnson, one of the practice GPs. I understand you want to speak to someone about your husband."

I explained our situation.

Pause.

"The earliest we can fit your husband in is on Friday."

In three days? No, I had not got this far to give up now. I played my last remaining card and took advantage of my role as a clinical researcher.

"Look, I'm a clinical scientist and work with doctors on a daily basis. My manager, also a doctor, has strongly advised me to get Ian referred for brain scans given his symptoms and negative blood results. I'm not leaving this surgery until someone starts taking us seriously."

Silence. My hands were trembling.

"OK, Mrs White, I will book your husband in this afternoon – it will have to be the last appointment of the day – and we shall then consider a referral."

"Thank you! Thank you!" I gushed, overcome with relief.

It took me a couple of attempts to place the receiver back in the cradle, my hands were shaking so much. Being assertive didn't come naturally to me, but I had to be strong to fight Ian's corner when he clearly couldn't. My sheer determination and unwavering love for the person who meant the world to me had at least moved us one step forward.

A few hours later, Ian and I returned to the surgery.

I had kept a written log of Ian's symptoms, appointments and medication and I brought this record with me to the appointment and relayed recent events. To my utter surprise, the GP seemed not to hear my information and proceeded to give Ian a brief examination.

"Given your continuing symptoms, Mr White, I have referred you for a brain scan," he announced. "These are generally reserved for patients with serious conditions like brain tumours."

I was dumbstruck. Was I really hearing this? Perhaps the exhaustion of the past few weeks was impacting my judgement, but something about his response angered me. I couldn't bite my tongue any longer. My husband had barely caused any expense to the health service after 41 years and on this one occasion he was going to be looked after. I would make damn sure of that. My eyes brimmed with unshed tears and a sob threatened to erupt from my throat as anger rose up within me.

"My husband is very ill," I started, trying to keep the wobble in my voice under control. "No one seems to have a clue what is going on despite blood tests and examinations. The prescribed tablets aren't working. Please believe me when I say we are not the kind of people to waste your time."

Despite my best efforts, my emotions were getting the better of me as tears slid down my cheeks. It had been a frustrating few weeks and his attitude was the final straw. I desperately wanted someone to understand how bloody serious this was.

""You're on the system as a fast-track referral so you should see a specialist within six weeks."

I sighed. Six weeks. Ian put his hand on my knee and squeezed it gently. We looked at each other, his eyes filled with concern.

"Thank you," he said quietly, and gently took my hand in his.

I couldn't help but glare at the doctor as we stood up to leave, but he was already busy shuffling papers on his desk, preparing for his next patient. This was someone whom I had seen for my own health issues in the past. We were of a similar age and he had always seemed approachable and helpful. Perhaps the fear I felt deep down about Ian's illness was clouding my ability to be rational, but I felt let down by the whole experience.

Chapter 12
Finally, a diagnosis

Thankfully, while I found the GP's attitude frustrating, he was as good as his word: only a week passed before Ian saw a neurologist. Ian now struggled to walk so I found a wheelchair in the hospital reception and manoeuvred him to the waiting area. At the allotted time, the consultant emerged from his room and I could tell from his expression as he saw Ian that he knew the cause of his problem – a look of understanding seemed to pass over his face. This is the difference between seeing a specialist, someone who regularly sees the same symptoms and conditions, and seeing our family doctor, who as a general practitioner can't be expected to know everything about all diseases.

I felt my stomach lurch as, once more, a feeling of unrest stirred deep within me, just as it had done on New Year's Eve. My gut instinct told me this medical professional would finally give us the answers we needed.

Encouraged by the consultant's approach so far, I sat down in the chair by his desk. I opened my notebook and described the events of the past few weeks, and this time I deliberately used clinical terminology: familiar words and phrases I knew from my work. I wanted him to know that we were not going to be messed about or treated like idiots. I needn't have worried. My intuition had been accurate. A true professional with confidence in his own ability, he was intrigued to know what I did for a living and treated us both with respect.

"Please go to the radiology department now, where you'll be seen immediately," he said.

Two minutes later, I wheeled my husband down the corridor to have his scans. Ian had a CT scan followed by an MRI.

"I know why they're doing the second scan," said Ian in a quiet voice as we waited together. He turned to look at me and I saw the worry and fear in his eyes. Goodness, he looked so small and vulnerable sat in that damn chair. "They're looking to see if 'it' has spread, aren't they?"

I took a deep intake of breath before answering. "I'm guessing it's just routine," I lied. "Precautionary – you know, so they have all the pictures at once."

My tone of voice gave it away.

"Fine actor you are," goaded the voice within me.

Of course, Ian was right. We were both thinking the same thing – 'it' being a tumour – but I couldn't bring myself to agree. In denial or not, I was determined that Ian was going to come through whatever it was that was causing his headaches.

We sat opposite the consultant as he reviewed the scans in front of him. Every sinew and muscle in my body was tense in anticipation of bad news. He looked gravely from Ian to me and then back to Ian.

"I'm afraid this is what I hoped it wasn't. You have a brain tumour."

I didn't hear anything else. The sound of his voice became distant as I took Ian's hand in mine and we looked at each other in utter disbelief. I was trying so hard not to cry that when the tears eventually broke through, an almighty sob erupted. This was so not part of our life plan. In that moment, our world disintegrated around us.

In stark contrast to the infuriatingly slow pace of the past few weeks, Ian was admitted onto a ward that same day. We were allowed home, briefly, for Ian to collect a few items and he insisted we visited the stables to say goodbye to his beloved Moose.

We drove in silence along the twisting country lanes from our home to the yard. Darkness was falling fast as we walked slowly over to Moose's stable. On hearing us, his beautiful chestnut face with its distinctive white blaze appeared over the door and he whickered a welcome. Ian patted Moose's golden neck and tenderly stroked his soft smooth nose.

"See you later, mate," he whispered and stroked Moose's face, lost in the moment.

They stood together like that for several minutes while I, once more, fought back the tears. I had to be strong.

"Dear diary, I can't believe I'm writing this...Ian has been diagnosed with a brain tumour. After weeks of feeling very tired, we ended up at A&E three weeks ago with him having a severe headache and vomiting. It's taken several GP appointments and a lot of stamping of feet to get him referred for a brain scan. The neurologist knew as soon as Ian shuffled into his room that it was serious. Tomorrow he has surgery to either remove the lesion or biopsy it. Dear God, let it be removed, benign and primary. This is sheer hell.

"God only knows what he's going through. He's a fighter – I truly believe we'll get through this together. I must be strong for him. Our family and friends have been incredible. I found it – still find it – very hard to accept help. Moose and Willow have been our emotional support. Just angels.

"Please look after Ian and bring him safely through this journey. I can't live without him – don't want to face life without him – won't live life without him because he's going to succeed in fighting this bastard lump that finds no place in Team White."

∞ ∞ ∞

Later that same day, Ian was settled in his bed on the ward. After a couple of hours, when I was sure he was fast asleep, I left quietly so as not to disturb him. Never had I felt so alone, and I am sure Ian felt the same.

In a couple of days, Ian was transferred to the neurological ward at the John Radcliffe Hospital near Oxford.

"I think we're going to have to get used to hospitals, my lovely," he said as I stroked his head and nodded.

"I think you're right, sweetheart," I replied. "But we'll fight this together. We're not going to be beaten."

A biopsy was needed to obtain a sample of the tumour and confirm what type of growth it was. The surgeons' aim was to remove the growth entirely and then tailor Ian's treatment to prevent its return. Brain surgery was imminent, but then we hit a problem.

"Dear diary, today has been the toughest one yet. I knew this week would be rough. The neurosurgeon told us today that Ian's tumour is too deep in the brain to be surgically removed. This means they can only take a sample, a biopsy, to see what type of cells the tumour contains. They'll then decide on treatment. The surgeon said, "if treatment is required…" And although I asked him to clarify what he meant, he didn't really. Having read up in my book about brain tumours, I know the prognosis isn't good. I can't help feeling we are losing the battle."

Although the neurosurgeon tried to reassure me, it wasn't working. My own brain was beginning to realise the consequences of not being able to operate. I sat there, stunned. Any hope I had of Ian's recovery was draining away fast. Had they told Ian the same information? I needed to see him.

Before I went, I contacted a friend of ours, someone whom we had known for a few years because he and his wife kept their horses at the same stables as us and who, now, became a fundamental part of keeping me, and Ian, reassured throughout what was to come. Neil was a doctor, and a highly experienced psychiatrist. On hearing about Ian's diagnosis, he had made it very clear to both of us that he was there if we had any questions.

I spoke to Neil every other day during those early few weeks. It is remarkable how kind people are during your darkest times and Neil was no exception. Looking back at our conversations now, I realised he never told me an untruth, but he never embellished the truth, either. He said as much as he needed to say about the procedures that Ian was going through and what the various specialists were telling us, but nothing more. He said enough to reassure us without raising panic. A skill indeed, and we were both very grateful for his support.

I jumped into the car and headed over to the hospital. An hour's drive, and I didn't remember any of it. Ian was pleased to see me and we sat chatting for a while before I tentatively raised the topic of surgery. It became clear to me that Ian knew he was having surgery to take a sample, but it was apparent he hadn't grasped that the tumour wouldn't be removed. He seemed in relatively good spirits now that he was being seen to and I hadn't the heart to dash his hopes. After all, maybe the doctors would be able to do more than they thought they could at the moment?

The next afternoon, I went with Ian's parents to the hospital so we could be there when he came out of theatre. We sat together in silence in the ward, helplessly united by the tragedy that was rapidly unfolding. There were no words.

Suddenly, the doors swung open and a team of nurses and doctors bustled in, wheeling Ian back onto the ward in his bed. An oxygen mask was strapped over his mouth and tubes lay all around him. It was quite a shocking sight and not for the faint-hearted. I held onto Pat, tightly, relieved to see Ian again but upset by how he looked.

Shortly afterwards, the patient occupying the bed opposite Ian was brought in having had his surgery. On seeing him, his poor wife collapsed to the floor – the sight was too much for her to bear.

Ian stayed in hospital for several more days to recuperate.

Whenever a nurse walked on to the ward, Ian asked the same question: "When can I go home?"

Every time he received the same response: "You won't be going anywhere until you drink more water."

He needed fluids to hydrate him and stabilise his heart rate and blood pressure. You have never seen a jug of water disappear so fast. When the nurses returned, Ian would hand them the empty container for a refill with a wry smile on his face.

"Look, all gone. Now can I get out of here?"

Needless to say, the nurses would laugh and refill it. Throughout this time, Ian never lost his sense of humour though it became darker as his illness progressed.

"Dear diary, please, please, please let Ian come through this. People do live with brain tumours if they're controlled. He's a fighter – and I just can't imagine life without him."

Chapter 13
Home comforts

At long last, Ian was well enough to come home while we waited for his treatment course to start. He rang me from the hospital as soon as his discharge was confirmed.

"I can escape," he said, clearly beside himself with excitement. "Come and get me as soon as you can."

We weren't out of the woods by any means, but despite the bigger picture I felt elated. This was going to be a great day and I sang along to the radio all the way to the hospital. I practically skipped into the waiting area, smiled at the receptionist and strode purposefully towards Ian's ward.

All the curtains were pulled around his bed.

Voices I didn't recognise drifted out from behind the screens.

Panic rose within me. Oh God. Had something happened to him in the time it had taken me to get here? My heart thudded. I returned to reception, a frown deeply engraved on my brow, and inquired as to the whereabouts of my husband.

"He's waiting for you in Room 312, down there," the receptionist responded, pointing her finger towards a long soulless corridor stretching away from the waiting room.

Thank goodness! I hurried towards my destination and tentatively knocked. No answer. I opened the door a little and peeked round. Empty. Where was he? I rang his mobile phone – no answer. What if he'd collapsed somewhere? What if he was now wandering about this vast building, confused, lost? I had to find him.

I walked faster and faster down each corridor, looking for open doors, anywhere where I might find my husband. Suddenly my phone rang, making me jump.

"Hi, it's me," said a hushed voice on the other end. "I'm in a room where they can't find me."

Ian guided me to his hiding place, as far away from reception as possible. He was so determined to come home, he wasn't taking any chances. I knew he was frightened – he clearly didn't want the doctors to find him and change their minds.

Over the next couple of weeks, we adopted a routine. Thanks to my incredibly understanding employers, I worked from home and was under no obligation to do very much. My project responsibilities were reduced and I was told to take as much time as I needed. I can't thank them enough for their kindness during this period.

Family and friends came over to visit us and we enjoyed going out for coffee and cake at local cafés. This was something we'd never done as a couple before. Ian loved cooking and baking, preferring to prepare food from scratch and eat at home.

One day, Ian and I ventured out to a nearby farm shop, a place we often passed but never visited. We sat under the pale oak beams of the converted barn, consuming the delicious fare, enjoying the ambience around us. Ian read the newspaper while I caught up on celebrity gossip in the magazine supplement.

I became aware of him staring at me, so I looked up.

"You OK?" I asked.

"Why haven't we done this more often?" was his response.

Good question. Our lives were busy: a mixture of working during the day and riding the horses in the evenings and at weekends. We never took time out to just 'be'.

I smile when I recall my paranoia about Ian eating too much cake. One of the side effects of his steroid medication was an increased appetite. Awareness of this made me determined to help him stay healthy and keep his weight down to give him the best chance of recovery. If I knew then what I know now, cake rations wouldn't have entered my mind – he could eat as much cake as he wanted.

Thankfully, Ian shared my determination for him to stay fit and healthy so we went out for strolls around the village whenever his tiredness levels allowed.

One sunny lunchtime we made our way slowly up our road. It was early spring – my favourite time of year. But today, I felt the fresh green buds on the trees and hedges, and the clumps of colourful daffodils, were mocking me with the irony of the season. Here was Mother Nature awakening from her winter slumber, showing signs of renewed growth and energy, which was in stark contrast to my husband's deteriorating health.

"We're very lucky to live here, aren't we?" Ian remarked as he followed me through the metal gate into the recreational ground.

It was true. We were fortunate to live in this beautiful rural community with acres of rolling countryside, picturesque villages and vibrant market towns.

"I still have so many things I want to do in life," he murmured, looking around him, taking in the views. "So many plans and ideas for the future."

Turning forty about eight months before had focused Ian's mind as to how he wanted to live the rest of his life. He planned to leave corporate life at fifty and, to satisfy his interest in antiques, he fancied becoming a furniture restorer. Since retiring, his father had enjoyed carpentry and we'd often find him in his workshop, whittling wood and making beautiful pieces of furniture for various members of the family. We received an old-fashioned chiming clock from him, which remains on our wall at home to this day.

"And you'll do them, my lovely," I replied. "We will fight every step of the way to get you there."

Yet every time I thought of the future, the only picture that came to mind was of a funeral – Ian's funeral. My head would shake automatically as if trying to remove this morbid scene from my thoughts. Perhaps this was my intuition, my subconscious, telling me what was to come, however hard I tried to push it away?

I believe now that my subconscious knew something bad was going to happen long before Ian's symptoms were noticeable.

About six months before Ian became notably ill, I was chatting to a colleague at work, putting the world to rights, as you do. She was a close friend as well as colleague so we usually opened up to each other about personal stuff. We were sharing our dreams for the future, and I remember describing to her how I usually saw a clear image in my mind of Ian and me standing in front of a white farmhouse surrounded by fields with hills in the background. A black Labrador sat by Ian's side and horses grazed in the neighbouring paddock.

"But recently, that picture has faded," I explained. "I now see myself sitting on my own, at a desk, writing. The walls around me are clad in white wooden panelling and I'm near water, like a river or the sea. I'm alone."

Why? Why was this happening? Neither of us could rationalise this change in vision.

Another 'omen' appeared when I walked through our garden to get to our driveway. A bird of prey, possibly a kestrel, swooped down in front of me and grabbed hold of a blackbird that had landed on the lawn. Drama unfolded as the squawking victim was carried off to his fate. I didn't realise the significance of that macabre event until after Ian's diagnosis.

Around the same time, Ian went to see his chiropractor for his three-monthly visit. He had suffered from a sore back for many years, but keeping active and riding the horses helped to keep the pain manageable.

"Goodness, have you fallen off your horse since you saw me last?" she remarked during this particular session.

"No," replied Ian. "Why?"

"Well, the whole left side of your body is way out of alignment, like it's experienced a significant trauma."

There was no plausible rationale for this at that time, but now I believe this was yet another sign that the tumour was present.

∞ ∞ ∞

Yet again, horses played an important role in our coping strategy. Some afternoons I would go up to the stables and ride to escape reality. Both our horses now lived out in a field full time to reduce costs and eliminate the need for frequent ridden exercise. I rode in the arena wearing my earphones, music pounding through my thoughts, blocking out my worries and anxiety.

Occasionally, Ian joined me if tiredness didn't get the better of him. Watching my once strong capable husband riding Moose at a slow walk was heart wrenching. The growth was located on the right side of Ian's brain and affected the left side of his body, including his vision. This explained the missed junctions on the M25 that day he returned from his business trip to Ireland. It also rendered his left arm weak so he couldn't grip the reins properly.

Moose looked after him, moving steadily around the arena. I swear our beautiful wise horse knew he had to look after his master and best friend. These afternoons, riding and being out in the fresh country air, gave Ian hope and joy. Simple pleasures certainly become more significant in these times of strife and Ian was grateful for every day he was able to visit the stables. I know it frustrated him that he could only 'plod around', but at least he was out there having a go.

Our equine friends became our therapists.

Ian was determined to remain involved with eventing so we went along to watch a one-day event at Tweseldown, a venue where we had both competed and where I knew one of our friends, Fiona, a professional photographer, was working that day.

Fiona was part of the team at the online magazine so our paths crossed regularly, not only when I was reporting from events as a journalist, but also when we were competing. She always looked out for us and, over the time we evented, captured many of our proud and special moments on film.

Fiona knew Ian was gravely ill, but hadn't seen him since his diagnosis. I'll never forget the look of concern that flickered across her face as she saw Ian's obvious frailty as we slowly made our way towards her on the cross-country course.

Ian followed just a stride or two behind me so I could act as his guide. Every step he took was an achievement and, true to form, he doggedly made it round most of the showground that day.

Having recovered from her initial shock, Fiona chatted away to us, asking after our horses and giving us an update on the day's action. The sky was a gunmetal grey, the low clouds releasing a steady relentless drizzle as we talked. I could see

Ian starting to shift his weight from one foot to another and I didn't want him to catch a chill.

That was the last time Fiona saw Ian.

We bid our farewells and made our way along the sandy tracks that crisscrossed through the bracken and gorse, characteristic of the Tweseldown landscape, back to the main courtyard, the hub of the event.

When we reached the brick quadrangle, where the various merchandise stands and coffee stalls were located, Ian suggested I bought hot drinks while he nipped to the gents. I watched as he picked his way gingerly over the wet cobblestones, glistening from the rain like precious gems, guiding him to the door, which was just out of sight.

A few minutes later, and unseen by me, Ian emerged from the toilet block. Having completely lost his bearings, he turned left instead of right. He wandered around the back of the old stables and barns feeling disorientated, unable to work out how to get back to the main square. Carefully carrying our coffees, I walked over to the toilet entrance, thinking Ian would be there waiting for me. I turned the corner and there was no sight of him. I called out his name. No reply. Where had he gone?

The courtyard itself wasn't big, but the site overall was several hundred acres with a busy main road twisting through it. I gulped down the fear and called his name again. Still no answer. Images of Ian having a seizure, lying face down and unable to stand, flashed into my mind and I shook my head as if to physically remove them.

My voice became high and trembling as I picked my way through the competitors and supporters milling around, calling out his name, my eyes scanning every nook and cranny. I randomly stopped people to ask them if they'd seen Ian, describing him as best I could. No sightings. I put the cups down on a nearby wall as tears pricked the corners of my eyes.

What the hell did I do now? Guilt washed over me: why hadn't I gone with him to make sure he was OK?

Then it came to me – the commentators. They could make an announcement over the tannoy. I turned and, as I did, spotted a familiar figure leaning against the red brick exterior of the end barn. His head was bowed. He looked utterly dejected.

"Ian. Oh God. Ian," I cried out, oblivious of the heads turning, curious to know who was shouting.

Placing the hot drinks on the floor, I ran over and reached my darling husband, whose face filled with recognition and relief. I embraced him with such gusto I nearly knocked him sideways.

"I'm frightened," he whispered. "Please – please don't lose me again."

His body shook as he cried, his face buried in my neck, and I held him and hugged him for dear life.

How the hell had our lives come to this? Only a month ago, we had been planning our eventing season, hoping to come here to compete Moose and Willow. My husband should have been galloping, fearlessly, astride his bold and eager eventer, negotiating a course of imposing timber obstacles. Yet here he was, scared beyond comprehension and unable to find his way back from the men's loos.

That incident still haunts me to this day.

∞ ∞ ∞

None of us really knows how we would cope when faced with a life-limiting condition and I admired the bravery and dignity with which Ian handled his fate. The one and only time he asked "Why me?" was the morning a parcel arrived from work.

The previous Christmas, I bought him a desk diary comprising photos from our last eventing season, Team White in action, which he'd placed in his office. Given his absence, a colleague kindly posted the calendar to him with a lovely note containing best wishes from all his team. I knelt by the side of the armchair as he sat and tore open the envelope.

Ian's face glistened with the tracks of his tears while he flicked through those pictures of happier times. Goodness, we had been blessed to have had a hobby that we were both so passionate about, that had given us precious time together as a couple and with his parents.

The arrival of this calendar stirred something within Ian, who, wiping his tears away, suggested we visited the weekly farmers' market in town. We hadn't been there since Ian's symptoms had worsened and I think we both needed to get out of the house and breathe in the fresh air of early spring.

We enjoyed strolling around the different stalls and bought some delicious treats we could cook for lunch. Ian pointed to a flower stand over in the corner and, with his arm linked through mine, we slowly and carefully made our way over. Having chosen a small bunch of tulips, a rainbow of bright reds, oranges and yellows, my favourite flowers, he handed them to me.

"I'm sorry we had to spend our wedding anniversary in hospital," he said, pausing for a few seconds to soothe the wobble in his voice. "These are for you, my lovely. Thank you for being with me, for being my wife."

I couldn't speak. Yet again, those words circled round in my mind: why us? Why Ian? Were we being punished for something we'd done, perhaps in a past life?

When we returned home, he asked me to book the cinema for that evening, while he went upstairs to bed to replenish his energy levels.

I remember our trip to the pictures vividly because it was the first time Ian showed any evidence of being self-conscious of his appearance and walking difficulties.

As we entered the brightly lit foyer, Ian, with his head bowed, said quietly, "Everyone is looking at me."

"Come on," I said, taking a tighter hold of his arm. "Everyone is too busy to even notice us."

We sat down in the theatre and 10 minutes later my husband was fast asleep, his head on my shoulder. I realised, with sadness, that Ian was fading and that at some point in the not too distant future, I faced life alone without this beautiful man beside me.

Chapter 14
Hope fades

After what seemed like an eternity, Ian received his biopsy results. We sat opposite the consultant and cancer nurse in a tiny room off the neurology ward as they relayed the information to us. His prognosis wasn't good. Ian had an aggressive type of brain tumour called a glioblastoma multiforme, or GBM, which was grade 4, the most severe level. Despite this devastating update, we desperately clung to the possibility that his illness would be adequately managed through radio- and chemotherapy, thus giving Ian an acceptable quality of life for a few years at least.

I still remember this day clearly, as if it were yesterday. We emerged from the meeting and took the lift down to the main hospital entrance in silence, both lost in our own thoughts, unable to audibly express our concerns.

We walked, our arms fitting together perfectly as we linked them in solidarity, through the shopping area, carefully negotiating those milling around the precinct: families and friends facing their own anguish and problems and hospital staff taking a well-earned break from the stress of their roles. I guided Ian towards the café where his parents were waiting for us, but before we got there, he stopped and turned to me. He didn't have to say anything. The desperation in his eyes said it all. We embraced, holding each other upright, our own life support. Goodness, how I loved this special man who had been my companion, confidante and cheerleader for almost 18 years, all my adult life.

Standing there, I felt everything go quiet, like we were in the peaceful centre of a storm, while the rest of the world whirled around us, our future plans being tossed out of the vortex, out of our control. We knew our time together was limited. Every single precious minute we had left was special.

"Dear diary, please let him be strong enough to start radiotherapy. Why is the approval for therapy taking so long to come through? Can you believe that when we finally get the go ahead, we may have to wait a few days for a bed to become available on the ward?

"Don't they understand that someone's life is at stake here?

"My darling Ian is going through hell and all I can do is give support. I wish with all my heart that I could wave a magic wand and make this dreadful thing go away."

Frustratingly, Ian's radiotherapy couldn't begin until his biopsy wound had sufficiently healed, which took at least six weeks – precious time Ian didn't have – and his irritation was palpable. Every time the phone rang, he asked if it was the hospital calling to say he could start treatment.

Another, unforeseen, factor delaying therapy was the fact we asked for a transfer to another hospital, closer to his parents, so they could take him to some of his appointments, thus enabling me to go into the office when needed. Unfortunately, this required a change in health trust and a chain of paperwork to be completed.

As the days went by, Ian's condition worsened, with epileptic seizures becoming a daily occurrence. I wasn't physically strong enough to hold him upright if he had a fit while standing and I didn't want him to fall and hit his head. He often involuntarily emptied his bladder during a seizure, too, which he found humiliating. We needed help so we moved in with his parents earlier than planned.

Finally, the transfer forms were approved and we went to see his cancer specialist with renewed optimism. Sadly, we experienced yet more exasperation when we were told his treatment had been deferred yet again, this time due to the seizures. Critically, each delay led to Ian losing confidence in his ability to fight and defeat this sodding tumour.

Living with his parents was tricky despite all the love and support we both gratefully received. I felt a million miles away from home and from my own family and friends. Exhaustion from worrying, caring and working were taking their toll. Ian's restlessness and craving for midnight snacks – another side effect of the steroids – meant he would go downstairs during the night to hunt out sustenance and I became tired and tetchy from sleep deprivation.

Usually, I accompanied him down the stairs to make sure he didn't fall. However, one night overwhelming tiredness enveloped my body. Selfishly, I pulled the duvet over my head as he opened the bedroom door to go downstairs alone. A few seconds passed and another door creaked open, followed by the sound of footsteps descending the stairs. I recognised his mum's tone as murmured voices spiralled up the stairwell. My heart sank as guilt, a frequent companion it seemed, filled my body. What a dreadful wife I felt for letting my husband risk falling down the stairs.

It was like we were children again. Understandably, his mum and dad wanted to care for their son, but I felt as if I was losing him as my husband.

Ian clearly understood my predicament because later that evening I sat on the bed while Ian lay under the duvet, too ill to sit downstairs in front of the fire with everyone else. I rested my head beside his on the pillow and he tenderly stroked my face with his hand.

"I know it's difficult for you living here, with Mum and Dad, but I want you to know that you're the reason I haven't jumped out of that window yet," he said quietly, as if he was reading my thoughts.

The following Sunday I drove back to our house, my refuge, leaving Ian with his mum and dad. I needed to pick up some additional clothes and other bits and pieces, but I also needed some space and to be at home, if only for a couple of hours.

Desperate to accompany me, Ian sat on the side of our bed, trying to get dressed.

"I'm coming with you," he said, as he grappled with his sock, a simple process made difficult by his condition.

"No, my darling, you have to stay here and rest. I won't be long. I just need to grab some bits and pieces."

He looked utterly crestfallen. I wanted him to come with me. I wanted to pack the car and drive back home, just the two of us, and spend whatever time we had left in our own house, but the logistics of Ian's care prevented us from doing just that. I steeled myself for my departure.

I had to do this for myself. I couldn't risk taking him. What if he had a seizure while I was driving? Besides, his parents would never have let him get in the car. I knew that. With a leaden heart, I drove out of their driveway.

Snowflakes spiralled in my headlights. Was insanity fogging my judgement? Travelling home when snow was forecast was surely madness, but I determinedly drove on. I felt compelled to make this journey. An hour later and I reached the familiar surroundings of our village. As I pulled onto our driveway, I heard the first few bars of our wedding song coming from the radio. I wept while resting my head on the steering wheel, listening to the theme tune to the happiest day of my life. What was happening to us? Tragedies didn't happen to ordinary people like me and Ian. Pessimism and a sense of foreboding overshadowed my usual positivity. If I'm honest, in that moment I fantasised about going back, picking up Ian, and driving to an isolated spot where we could fill the car with exhaust fumes and end this misery once and for all. Ian was my life and I couldn't imagine continuing without him.

I prised myself from my seat and welcomed a sense of relief as I walked into our cottage. What a comfort it was to be back in our home. This was our refuge from the world. I fell in love with this cottage and her cosy period charm the minute we walked in on the day of our first viewing, but Ian had played it cool.

"Those sash windows will let in a hell of draught in the winter," he warned as we walked around, appreciating the light that flooded into each room and admiring the Victorian fireplaces.

"Oh, I know that, but can we still buy her? Please," I implored. "I'll wear extra layers. I won't mention the cold."

I had a battle on my hands given the price was at the top of our budget and some renovation work was needed upstairs. We consulted a local builder, who surveyed the property, and, on receipt of his cost estimate, we decided to walk away. Nothing more was said until a few days later, when the estate agent rang me and asked if we wanted to make an offer.

"We do love the house," I explained. "But given the building work required, we'd have to put in a very cheeky offer to afford it."

"Try me."

I took a deep breath and gave her the price we were willing to pay. I screwed my eyes up, waiting for her to laugh and say, "are you serious?"

"Actually, you're not far off the mark. The vendor wants a quick sale as she's already bought somewhere else. I shall put your offer to her and get back to you as soon as possible."

What? My eyes popped open in surprise. I stuttered a thank you and quickly rang Ian to relay the news.

The next morning, the estate agent rang to confirm our offer had been accepted and within a month we moved into our cottage.

The living room clock chimed and my thoughts were jolted back to the present moment. Time for me to return to Ian. I needed to be with him again. The snow flurry hadn't lasted and I made it back in time for supper. Hearing about Ian's day, I realised my absence had given his family precious time together without me, which soothed my feelings of guilt.

The next evening after dinner, we all congregated in the living room to watch TV. But before long, I became aware of Ian fidgeting. I glanced across at him. His face was flushed red and he looked uncomfortable.

"Are you too hot?" I asked. "Why don't you take off your hat?"

He had taken to wearing a woolly hat all day every day because he complained of his head being cold. I also think he believed it would protect his biopsy scar from any infection.

"My head feels really sore," he said, trying to find the wound with his fingers.

"Let me see."

I gently parted his hair where I knew the wound was and when I saw the angry swollen scar tissue, my heart sank. He needed medical attention and fast if he stood any chance of starting treatment any time soon. I didn't want him to go into hospital any more than he did, but I knew it was critical for him to get specialist care.

The ambulance pulled into the driveway. The bright headlights sweeping through the windows alerted us to its arrival. I helped Ian up from his chair and he walked gingerly towards the front door.

"Make way, dead man walking. Dead man walking," he announced.

Gallows humour. I hated hearing him say this, probably because I knew his words were so close to the truth and I was frightened. I couldn't tell him to stop because I knew this was his way of coping.

I accompanied him to the hospital, with his parents following behind in the car. He was admitted and the nursing staff made him comfortable and attended to his infected wound.

The following day I finished work at lunchtime, eager to visit Ian and stay with him for the rest of the day. The sun was shining and I felt hopeful. I couldn't wait to see him. I hated the fact we were apart yet again. I got into the car and my phone immediately rang. Pat. Cold fingers of fear closed themselves around me, filling me with dread.

"Come home, darling," she said in hushed tones.

"But I'm on my way to the hospital," I explained, feeling a little put out that she seemed to be preventing me from seeing my husband.

"Come home – please," she repeated. "We need you to come home first."

I sighed. OK, I'd go home, as instructed, but then dash back to the hospital to see Ian.

His mum and dad were waiting for me at their front door as I pulled up, their faces etched with worry.

"He's unconscious."

I collapsed into his dad's arms.

"No," I kept saying, over and over, as his dad held me tightly, trying to keep me upright.

"I want to see Ian. I want to be with him," I sobbed.

We arrived at the hospital to be greeted by Ian's consultant, whom we followed down a cold, sterile corridor to his office; all of us were afraid of what we were going to hear. I felt like I was acting in a TV drama; it was all too surreal and difficult to comprehend.

"Dear diary, Ian's condition deteriorated yesterday. His parents visited him in the morning and they couldn't wake him up. The nurses were called and everyone is now trying to get him well enough to start treatment. I spent the night with him. The increased steroid dose has had some effect and he recognised my voice. He squeezed my hand and spoke a little. Goodness, how quickly life can change. Come on Ian, keep fighting, my lovely. Keep hold of your dreams."

"Ian's tumour has grown. It's now the size of a grapefruit and I'm afraid he's too ill to receive any treatment," the doctor explained. "He needs to stay here, under observation, until his condition stabilises."

What? I couldn't believe what I was hearing. I stared at the floor, at the cold charmless tiles, as thoughts swirled around my head. We were a normal happy family, living our lives. Ian was 41, for God's sake. We had created a wonderful life together, finally earning enough money to realise our dreams after years of building our careers from students.

That was it. No more. Ian was a good man with his life ahead of him. Why? Why was this happening to us? I felt everything pause, waiting for my reaction. Like an audience hushed into silence as the drama before them reached its climax. Then anger and grief exploded from me.

"No! No! No!" I screamed, stamping my feet, over and over, sobbing hysterically, my fists clenched in defiance. "I'm not going to let him die!"

Ian's parents wrapped their arms around me to console me as we all tried to come to terms with this latest news. At that moment, I wished with all my heart that this was a scene from a movie and someone else was in our shoes.

We sat by Ian's bedside for the rest of that day, while he lay there unaware of our presence.

I stroked his head and took his hand in mine, willing him to come round.

"Hang on," I thought. "Something isn't right. There's something missing. His wedding ring."

I stood up in a panic. I knew this was a sign – another bad omen. I looked around, scanning the ward for a nurse, a doctor, anyone who could tell me where his ring had gone. A nurse walked in. I ran over and quickly grabbed her, bringing her back to Ian's bed.

"Look," I said, pointing at his ringless finger, my voice rising as anxiety soared.

"His wedding ring has gone. Where has it gone?"

The nurse looked as shocked as I felt.

"They may have taken it off while he had his scans this morning, but it should have been put back or stored in a safe place. Let me go and find someone to ask," she said before hurrying off.

She came back with a colleague, who looked at me apologetically before walking towards the bin next to Ian's bed.

"What on earth is going on?" I asked, my voice trembling with fury.

I couldn't believe what I was seeing. The contents of the bin were emptied on the floor and after a lot of searching among the bits of paper and debris, the ring was found. Profuse apologies followed, but I was too angry to speak and placed the precious gold band in my pocket for safekeeping.

Ian's mum and dad suggested I went home with them later that evening to rest, but I wanted to stay. They understood and left me there, promising to come back early the next day or earlier, if Ian came round.

I sat in the chair beside his bed all night, my head dropping as sleep found me periodically. My whole body ached the next morning, but it was all worthwhile when I heard Ian moan and move his head. A nearby nurse bustled over.

"Is Kathryn here?" he asked her. "Kathryn – is she here?"

She smiled and nodded as I took his hand in mine.

"I'm here, sweetheart. I'm here. I'm not going anywhere."

He managed a weak smile before his eyes fluttered shut and then opened again as if he was double-checking I was still there. My whole body flooded with relief and so much love for this dear man, my best friend, who was fighting the biggest battle of his life.

"Dear diary, Ian is exhausted. I worry that our visits are tiring him. I am also tired, and angry, at being in such a hopeless situation. I don't feel like we are husband and wife anymore and I find myself resenting sharing him with his family, which I know is selfish.

"I was hoping to be greeted by a brighter Ian this morning, but sadly not. He'd wet his bed during the night. His t-shirt was soaked and he told me he was struggling. All morning he slept while I read the paper. Feeding him this lunchtime was tricky. He's hungry, but lacks the energy to eat. I desperately want to have conversations with Ian about our plans for the future, yet I haven't had a proper chat with my husband for days now."

Chapter 15
That scary word

"*D*ear diary, the nurse's 'knowing look' when I departed this afternoon frightened me. You always try to dismiss the signs, but in your heart, deep down, you're always aware of the reality. Please look after Ian. Please let him be the one who shows us that this tumour can be beaten – please."

Ian spent the next two weeks in that hospital ward and remained conscious throughout, though he slept a lot. I spent every day with him, arriving first thing and leaving late evening. The staff did their best but were run off their feet so I fed Ian at mealtimes as he was too weak and uncoordinated to feed himself.

A physiotherapist visited us a couple of times to give Ian some exercises to do to see if we could get him strong enough for treatment. I remember some shred of optimism returning the day Ian managed to shuffle, albeit with me and the physio either side of him, to the bathroom, but that would be the only occasion he did so. He had a catheter fitted, but required help to get to the toilet for bowel movements. I became his carer and, though our love for each other was clear for anyone to see, the balance of our relationship had shifted. In such a public environment, and with all the tubes and wires around him, I didn't feel able to lie on the bed beside him just to give him a hug and reassurance.

"Dear diary, I spent the afternoon and most of the evening with Ian today. He was extremely tired. I worry our visits are exhausting for him. When I arrived on the ward, the nurses said he'd been quite chatty earlier and had been telling them all about 'his Whitey'. He managed to sit in the chair beside his bed for supper. Partway through, he told me he needed the toilet, but I couldn't get hold of any of the nurses in time to help me take him to the bathroom so he defecated in his pants. My heart breaks for him. I know how humiliated he feels – it's emasculating. I cleaned up while Ian just said sorry over and over."

His family visited each day and were very generous and respectful about giving us time together. Friends came to call, too, and insisted I left the ward to have some lunch or at least something to drink.

Every evening, Pat kept my dinner warm for me in the oven for when I returned home. Both his parents would sit with me in the living room to hear my updates. I don't honestly know how we all survived. I think our absolute love for Ian and each other kept us going.

And Ian kept his sense of humour even in these darkest of times.

One morning, 4 am to be precise, my mobile phone rang. Ian. I buried myself under the duvet, worried about disturbing his sleeping parents in the room next door.

"Hello, it's me," he whispered.

My heart skipped a beat hearing his voice even at that early hour.

"Hello, my lovely," I replied. "Are you OK?"

"No," was the response. "I've been ringing my alarm and no-one is coming. I need to go to the toilet and no-one is coming."

"OK, OK," I soothed. I sensed his anxiety. "Leave it with me."

I rang off and immediately called the ward phone number. A very grumpy female voice answered, clearly unimpressed at receiving an outside call at this hour. Undeterred, I explained that my husband was in need of urgent assistance for the toilet.

"He has a catheter fitted, but I'm worried it hasn't been emptied – he had a wet bed yesterday morning when I arrived."

Her reply was abrupt, but she assured me that someone would go to Ian's aid. I wasn't convinced, but a few minutes later my phone rang again.

"You grass," Ian laughed, clearly relieved at being relieved.

Despite all he faced, Ian never stopped worrying about me. One evening I drove to the hospital, having nipped out to do some errands while Ian slept. Having been stuck in rush hour traffic I arrived flustered and frustrated, but sat down beside Ian and said nothing about my experience. However, my exasperation hadn't gone unnoticed.

When I reached the door to leave later, he called out, "Please take care driving home, won't you, my lovely?"

My precious man was more concerned about my safety than his own precarious situation.

"Dear diary, Ian's mum told me that when she visited him today in hospital, Ian kept asking where I was. When she came back from getting coffee, he said, 'Have you seen Whitey down there?' Hearing this fills me with compassion for my darling, beautiful husband. I know he loves me so much and I miss him dreadfully when I'm not there with him."

When Ian had been assessed by the physiotherapist, the oncologist decided that treatment wasn't an option. The decision hit Ian hard. I saw the fire go out of his belly that day and he became quieter and more withdrawn.

Determinedly, I clung on to the hope that he would keep rallying and eventually come home. I couldn't allow myself to think of the alternative. But that all changed when a Macmillan nurse came to see me.

I was ushered into a characterless room off the ward where there was a beige sofa and armchairs. For the first time since Ian's diagnosis, the word 'terminal' was used to describe his condition. He was in a lot of pain, particularly in his neck. The hospital staff was struggling to provide him with adequate relief. His mum and I regularly brought in hot lavender pads to try and ease his discomfort.

"He needs stronger medication and more intensive care," explained the Macmillan nurse, quietly, sensitive to my reaction. "We need to transfer him to a hospice."

My heart plummeted and I sank back in the chair, covering my face with my hands as I tried to come to terms with what I'd just heard. Hospice. A word filled with such negative connotations.

"But he's having physiotherapy. He'll get fitter and well enough for treatment, won't he?" I sounded like a small, frightened child.

The nurse shook her head and handed me tissues as tears spilled once more down my cheeks.

Two days later, on 4 April, paramedics wheeled Ian out of the ward on an ambulance trolley. The nurses cried and gave me hugs goodbye. Ian had been popular with many of the nursing staff, probably because he was relatively young and they'd seen us together and with our family every day. I guess they also knew the end was near.

I followed the ambulance through the Oxfordshire countryside, feeling dejected, and thankful for the distraction that driving brought. We arrived at the Sue Ryder hospice located in the beautiful village of Nettlebed. Built in the early 1900's and in the style of a traditional manor house, the hospice was a stunning location and the former home of Ian Fleming, author of the James Bond stories, and his family. Set in extensive gardens, surrounded by picturesque rolling countryside, it seemed a fitting place for Ian, a countryman at heart, to end his days.

The double-height entrance hall housed an imposing stone fireplace. Dark wooden panels lined the walls and a sweeping staircase led up to the wards. While the nurses settled Ian into his room, a doctor, a woman not much older than me with a kind face and gentle manner, guided me back downstairs to a small office where I immediately noticed the numerous boxes of tissues scattered around on every available surface. I curled my hands into fists, pressing my nails into my palms and bit my lower lip, hard.

"They're not going to get me," I thought. "I – am - not - going - to - cry."

Five minutes later, I gulped for air and reached for yet another tissue as my body shuddered with emotional release.

"Ian is gravely ill. Our priority will be to make him as comfortable as possible."

I nodded, unable to speak or look up.

"He doesn't have long now, Kathryn," she said gently. "He has days rather than weeks."

I closed my eyes and took a deep breath, inhaling the musty air tinged with the smell of disinfectant. What I would have done to have swapped chairs with her that day, for my life to return to some kind of normality – even mundane, I'd settle for that. Anything but this living hell.

I didn't want to watch my husband deteriorate over months or years with no quality of life or hope of any respite. He was an active person who loved being outdoors. Well, life could be very cruel – and here it was in its cruellest form. There was nothing anyone could do to make my Ian better. All we had left in our armoury was the ability to ease his pain and make his last few days bearable. Within an hour or so of his arrival, Ian's pain was finally soothed and we witnessed a glimpse of humour return.

I placed some of his belongings on top of the cabinet next to his bed and one of the nurses remarked on the rosette I displayed by the water jug.

"I won that on my horse, Moose," Ian said, smiling proudly. "At Gatcombe Horse Trials."

"The home of Princess Anne," I added.

"This hand," continued Ian, now holding up his right hand, his mouth curling into a cheeky grin, "has touched royalty."

He winked at the nurse, who was laughing while she tucked in the bed sheets.

"I'll remember that when I give you a wash, then," she responded.

I stayed full time and had a camp bed to sleep on next to Ian. This was replaced by a bed when he moved into a beautiful private room, which was light and airy thanks to the large mullioned windows overlooking the gardens and pond. At night, I would wheel my bed next to Ian's. Given the privacy we had, I could lie next to him, with my arms around him. We could be husband and wife once more.

"Dear diary, another precious day with Ian. I went for a walk around the hospice grounds today and spotted a beautiful hare bounding towards the hedgerow and a small herd of deer grazing in the fields beyond. The countryside is where I belong. I miss being able to talk to Ian. I feel our privacy has been cruelly invaded by family and medical staff, though I know they are all doing their best to support us both. That's all for now. I feel exhausted and very sad."

I was exhausted, vulnerable and helpless, and I gratefully embraced the endless love and care given to us both by the hospice team. Staying here erased my fear of hospices. What truly wonderful places they are, where kind and compassionate people carry out their remarkable work. The nurses had sufficient time and resources to provide five-star care. When we pressed the alarm for attention, someone was with us in minutes, day or night. Not only did they look after Ian, they also looked after me and our families. I had three meals a day and the nurses ensured I stayed well hydrated with tea and coffee.

"Dear diary, being here at the hospice is like being in a protective and supportive bubble. If I venture outside, I feel alienated from the rest of the world. I don't share the happiness of everyone around me. The grim reality is hard to bear. Stepping over the threshold of our cottage on my own will be heart-breaking."

My only contact with the outside world was my morning walk to the village post office to pick up a newspaper. Every time I walked through the tunnel of trees that led me to the village and the 'real world', I'd have a conversation in my head with Ian's granny, who had passed away a year before.

"You're not having him yet," I'd mutter after Ian had survived another night.

Mid-morning, I'd retreat downstairs while Ian had a bed wash or was attended to by the medical team to check his morphine supply.

The family room, with coffee-making facilities and jigsaw puzzles, became my sanctuary. Fitting those cardboard pieces together kept me sane as I became absorbed in the activity, completely taking my mind off the reality of our situation. I was acutely aware that in days I would be bereft of my soulmate.

One lunchtime I felt a dire need to escape the confines of Ian's room and his parents, who had dropped by. That particular day, I felt unsociable and low. Where could I go? At that moment, a woman with a lovely cheerful face peered round the door.

"Hello. Anyone need a back massage?" she asked.

Not a question any of us expected, but without hesitation my hand shot up.

"Me."

Actually, did I say woman? I mean angel who specialised in aromatherapy and massage. I followed her to the treatment room, a small square space which must have been south facing as I recall the sun streaming in through the window. We sat down on two plastic chairs placed facing each other.

"How are you feeling?" she asked gently, her eyes reflecting the kindness within.

My bottom lip wobbled. Oh, this was going to be messy.

She handed me a tissue as the flood gates opened and moved her chair closer so she could wrap her arms around me. I welcomed the warmth of her body, feeling safe and protected from the horror unfolding.

As my sobs subsided she gently guided me over to the massage table, where I lay face down looking through the little port hole at the floor below. Slowly, her warm hands moved over my bare skin, easing the knots and unleashing yet more suppressed feelings. My nakedness felt appropriate – I had nowhere to hide – I needed to accept the truth and face what was coming.

My body shook with each emotional discharge, my muscles relishing the chance to stretch and let go of tension. A smell of soothing lavender from the oil she used surrounded me, relaxing my mind.

Despite the hideous tragedy unfolding around me, that massage felt incredible.

Sitting back in the chair afterwards, I described everything that had happened over the past few months, welcoming the release of not having to put on a façade of being strong.

Listening intently to my story, she said, "I think it's important you say goodbye to Ian. Tell him how you feel, from the heart."

She was right, of course. I will be forever grateful for that piece of advice. I had been putting on a brave face, staying strong, too frightened to acknowledge Ian's prognosis and let him go. Now I knew I needed to tell him how much he meant to me and how much I loved him before he passed away.

I returned to Ian's room and found him lying alone in his bed, his parents having already left. Carefully, I lay down beside him, placing my arm gently over his chest. I wanted him to know; to sense I was there with him. He was permanently connected to a syringe driver containing a cocktail of drugs so he was barely conscious and speech was difficult.

Taking a deep breath, I opened my mouth and let the words spill out. I told him how he had changed my life for the better. Together, we had created a life we both loved. We were a team.

"Team White will live on forever," I whispered in his ear. "We certainly have some beautiful memories. I love you, my darling, and always will."

He lightly squeezed my hand and I wriggled closer to him as he tried to clear his throat. A gargled noise followed. He was trying to speak. I didn't catch it all but I heard one word: 'perfect'. I let my tears fall silently as I lay there, my frail husband in my arms, cherishing a beautiful poignant moment with my best friend.

"Dear diary, I hope Ian feels his life has been a triumph. I am extremely privileged to have shared my life with such a man – a genuine person who I know loves me as much as I love him. It's going to be so bloody difficult living without him but he will always be with me."

That afternoon Moose himself visited the hospice to say his goodbyes, thanks to the generosity of our friend John. He transported our horse an hour and a half to Nettlebed so Ian could say goodbye to him.

Ellie, head girl from the yard, accompanied him. Throughout the early stages of Ian's illness, Ellie had been a rock for me. She helped me exercise our two horses and many a time, while out on a ride, she had listened and offered comforting words when I broke down in sadness or anger. She was, and remains, a great mate of mine.

Having an equine visitor was a first for the hospice. Cats and dogs often visited their owners, but never a horse.

My legs gave way when John lowered the ramp and I saw Moose, such was the relief at seeing his familiar face. I hadn't appreciated how far away from home I felt, having thrown myself into the daily routine of caring for Ian. Goodness, how I missed my friends.

We led Moose round to the gardens close to Ian's room, where the nurses had placed his bed close to the open window. He stood still and angelic, as if he knew the significance of his visit, to say farewell to his master and friend.

I believe our hearing is the last of our senses to go before we die so although my dear husband was comatose and unable to communicate with us, I felt confident he still knew what was happening. The nurses who were with him kept up a running commentary and they told me afterwards how he wriggled his feet ever so slightly when they said 'Moose'.

While Ellie loaded him back onto the horsebox, John came up to Ian's room with me. I'll never forget how tenderly he spoke to Ian and I hope his voice was a reassuring and familiar sound from home. He sat by the bed and chatted about everyday stuff, telling Ian how the horses were doing and what he and his sons, all accomplished horsemen in their own right, had been up to.

When he stood up to leave, this dear man placed his hand gently on Ian's head and quietly said, "see you later, mate."

A year on, quite unbelievably, John suffered exactly the same type of brain tumour as Ian and died within a few months of diagnosis. One good thing that came out of mine and Ian's experience with our GP is that the surgery reacted quickly to John's symptoms and immediately referred him for a scan. Sadly, John knew what he faced having watched Ian's illness progress and I saw the fear in his face when he shared his diagnosis with me. John was a gentle, kind man, especially around the horses; a real country character who is missed by everyone in our equestrian community.

"Dear diary, Ian is still with me, but he has not eaten for a couple of days now and the nurses have told me that we are in the final stages of my darling husband's life. He is struggling with phlegm rattling away in his throat. The 'death rattle', they call it. It breaks

my heart to think our journey is coming to a close. I dread living without my darling Ian; not being able to share life's ups and downs, or having a hug whenever I need one. I don't think I'll ever understand why he's been so cruelly taken from us.

"Please let Ian go peacefully, in the night, in his sleep, just the two of us together to the end."

On 15 April 2008, a couple of days after Moose's visit, my soulmate gave up his fight and passed away – just nine weeks from that first visit to the consultant. The nursing staff warned me that patients choose their time to let go, sometimes passing away when their loved ones have left the room. That day, Ian's breathing had become erratic and his facial expression had changed such that he was almost unrecognisable.

Ian took his last breath with me by his side, but only just.

I had been discussing a concern I had with one of the nurses, whose office was a few doors down the corridor. Feeling reassured, we both walked back to Ian's room. As we entered, he took a loud rasping breath followed by ghastly stillness. My hands flew to my face. I dashed to his bedside, howling, while the nurse quietly closed the door to give us privacy.

I had to vacate the room that evening so I returned home with Natalie, a work colleague of Ian and friend who had visited us several times during his illness. We hadn't known her for more than a couple of years, but she had been an incredible support to both of us during those last few months. Her nursing background and personal experience of loss and serious illness gave her a unique insight into our predicament. She understood how exhausting it is to be a carer and how all attention is focused on the patient so she always remembered to check I was OK as well as Ian.

"Dear Ian [after Ian died, I found it comforting to write my diary as if I was speaking to him directly], today is the first day of a new period in my life and I'm not sure I can face it. You left me yesterday and I know you were taken from all the people you love. Thank you for allowing me to be there when you took your last breath. I feel so peaceful in our home. I feel you all around me. My deep, deep frustration is that I can no longer feel you physically or have a laugh like we used to. I miss you dreadfully. The pain is unbearable. But I will be strong – for you, my love – and try to be kind, generous and sunshiny – because I know you love me for those qualities."

I didn't sleep at all well, despite intense tiredness, as grief burned at my throat. I tried to breathe it away, but couldn't. Exhausted and numb, I walked about the house the next morning in a daze, unable to focus, while Natalie busied herself making breakfast. I walked into the kitchen and it was then that I saw them. There on the table were Ian's reading glasses.

He'd worn them more frequently over the past year, perhaps another sign of the growth in his brain. I picked up the delicate frames and held them in silence as I recalled the day we had gone to collect them from the opticians. We walked out of the shop into the busy mall where he carefully placed his brand-new spectacles on his nose, eager to see the effects. He wasn't disappointed.

"Bloody hell!" he exclaimed as he looked up and down the thoroughfare. "I can see Marks and Spencer's."

The store was right down at the end of the shopping centre and the green illuminated letters shone out. Previously a blur to Ian, the sign was now in sharp focus.

I smiled through the tears as I placed them back on the table, and sighed. I needed to see our horses. They were my family and I needed to be with them.

Natalie and I walked onto the yard and a few people came over to give me a hug, including Ellie; a couple melted into the background, unsure how to react.

We continued down the muddy track that ran between the fields and as we rounded the corner, I saw my beautiful Moose and Willow, waiting by the fence, their ears pricked, eager to say hello. My legs buckled as the enormity of what had happened ripped through me. I rocked, back and forth on the floor, my head in my hands, with Natalie holding me, letting me release the agonising grief and sadness that flowed from me.

My life had changed beyond comprehension. I couldn't bear it. I was a widow, a widow at 37, and I would never see my Ian again.

Chapter 16
Blooms of doom

*"D*ear Ian, the cards and flowers are beautiful. You were highly thought of and very much loved. Everyone is so shocked and saddened. "I miss you so much it hurts. I wake up each morning wishing with all my heart that I'll find you lying next to me. Everyone who tells me I'm being strong doesn't see me in the morning – when the nightmare becomes reality. It's like Groundhog Day, the horror movie. I would do anything to have you back. Even just for an hour, 30 minutes, hell, just a few seconds. I want to touch you, smell you, kiss you. I can't last a lifetime without you beside me. We were meant to grow old together."*

Flowers and sympathy cards. The normal stuff we've all sent to those who have suffered bereavement, to show how much we care. Being on the receiving end, those flowers and cards take on a whole different meaning. They act as a stark reminder of the truth you don't want to acknowledge.

The first bouquet arrived a couple of days after Ian's death. The blooms were a glorious bright yellow, my favourite colour. Despite their beauty and the love with which they were sent, they conveyed the terrible truth. My husband was dead and here was the proof. Of course, the arrival of one means more are on their way, each one sent with so much affection. How can a house full of stunning flowers be one of so much sadness?

The time between Ian dying and his funeral sped by in a complete and utter haze. My mum came to stay and she was an absolute godsend. Each morning I would wake up and for a split second everything seemed fine until the debilitating agony flooded my senses. Pulling the duvet over my head, I'd curl up into a ball, hoping that I'd wake up again and all would be back to how it had been, with Ian by my side.

Mum would bring me a cup of tea before coaxing me out of the bed and downstairs. I sat, still in my dressing gown, staring into the distance, unable to speak, not wanting anything to eat. I sensed her feeling of helplessness, but I couldn't shake off the raw grief gnawing away inside me. I don't honestly think I would have made it through those first couple of weeks without my mum's company. Even with her there, the house seemed deathly quiet, as if everything within had become still out of respect.

Numerous messages of sympathy came by email from the eventing community and especially from readers of our Team White column. The compassion really touched me. Ian's death even made it into the online discussion forum of *Horse and Hound Magazine* (the legend that it is). Despite being a private man, I know Ian would have been heartened by the love received from our equestrian family.

"Dear Kathryn, I was saddened and shocked to learn the news about Ian. I have enjoyed reading your column over the years, they always made me laugh. When you started writing them, my husband also evented. It was so nice to know that there were other couples as mad as us, who, like us, had their ups and downs. Like Moose, my husband's horse also has an aversion to dressage. I remember reading your report after you had been to Gatcombe and Moose won his first novice point. That really spurred us on. It's all very well reading about Olympic hopefuls, but you and Ian were a source of encouragement for grassroot riders, which, let's be honest, accounts for 90% of British Eventing members. Thinking of you at this sad time."

Tribute from reader of Team White column.

"Dear Kathryn. Although we never met, through your Team White column I do feel as if I have come to know you both. As an amateur rider struggling to improve, I felt that I could relate to your trials and tribulations. I too, like Ian, have struggled to improve my dressage. Nothing I can say will make it any easier, but I, for one, will miss him and I can therefore only imagine what it must be like for you and those close to him."

Tribute from reader of Team White column.

In spirit, as in life, Ian still managed to make me laugh with his wicked sense of humour, as this next story illustrates.

Funeral arrangements kept my mind occupied. Mum and I visited the local undertakers to finalise plans and sign paperwork. I had had to take some of Ian's clothes along for them to dress his body, which now lay in the chapel of rest. Mum accompanied me when I went along to say goodbye once more. I had never done this before and, though I have no regrets about seeing Ian, I will never do it again for anyone else. The corpse lying in the coffin looked nothing like my Ian. When I recall that moment, even now, I get a gnawing pain deep in my stomach. I have to inhale, deeply and slowly, and then exhale quickly, a rush of air escaping my lips, as if expelling the image from my being.

I placed three tulips beside him, picked that morning from our garden, one each for 'I love you', and a handwritten note.

After our appointment, we stepped out onto the pavement and I put my arm through Mum's as we walked back to the carpark.

"I don't believe it," I suddenly exclaimed as we walked down the line of cars, my hand flying to my mouth in shock.

I quickened my pace towards the traffic warden standing by my car, busily writing in her pad.

"Bloody hell, she's going to give me a parking ticket."

My breath was coming out short and fast as I reached her.

"Please, please don't give me that ticket," I pleaded, quickly glancing at my watch.

I tapped its face with my index finger, showing the time to the woman standing in front of me, now hurriedly ripping the completed ticket from her pad.

"Please," I implored. "We're only a couple of minutes over and I've just come from the funeral place. My husband has died, and..."

My voice tailed off, silenced by sobs rising up in my throat.

"Sorry, madam," she replied, tearing the offending sheet along the perforations. "I've written it now so I'll have to give it to you. I suggest you contact the number that's written on there and ask them to revoke it."

How I stopped myself from grabbing the ticket and ripping it up, I don't know, but I remained polite.

"Thanks," I said, through gritted teeth, and turned to unlock the driver's door.

I felt this ridiculous farce was a little reminder that Ian's spirit was with me. This was typical 'Mr White humour', and I could see him sat on his cloud, supping on a large brandy, his shoulders bouncing up and down as they always did when he had a fit of giggles.

Under my breath I muttered, "Ian White, this is NOT funny!", but I did manage a little smile as I felt the connection with him deep inside me.

"Dear Ian, I believe you're having a laugh at my expense. I got a parking fine today. Was that your doing? Well, I've had my revenge. I bought that candy-striped teapot you didn't like from our favourite tea shop afterwards – and the matching milk jug!"

This strong feeling I had of him being with me helped me deal with this and other hurdles that were to come. What I had just been through put this latest challenge into perspective – a parking ticket was hardly life and death, after all. In the end the council took note of my written plea and didn't cash my cheque.

∞ ∞ ∞

Nothing prepares you for the sight of a hearse pulling up outside your home carrying your husband's body.

So many of our friends and family paid their respects, including two friends who travelled all the way from Norway, friends we had made during our riding holidays in Galway.

"Rest in peace, mate. A man among boys. Thank you for keeping an eye on me through our university years. It only seems like yesterday. Great days, which I often reminisce about with great fondness."

Tribute from a university friend.

Once more, Ian was going to have some fun from beyond the grave, this time in the crematorium service.

According to the eulogy, written by a friend of his, Ian's talent as an event rider extended to competing in the prestigious Badminton International Horse Trials, riding around one of the biggest courses in the world.

"In your dreams, Mr White," I thought with a weak smile as I glanced across at our friend from the stables, John, who raised his eyebrows in surprise.

"It always seems that the people that have the most to offer in life are the ones that are taken away far too soon. I will always have an image of Ian on his lovely horse, Moose, with a big grin on his face as they finished yet another brilliant cross-country round. Although they were never going to win team medals, Ian and Moose typified for many what our sport is all about – the partnership between rider and horse and a huge enthusiasm for the sport of eventing."

Many of our friends and family came back to our local pub for the wake – the same one where Ian and I had spent our Friday nights planning our weekends only a few months before. The whole event, from start to finish, was extraordinary. It sounds bizarre to say this, but I felt like I was buzzing the entire day. Even when I got dressed in the morning and looked at the reflection in the mirror, I felt surrounded by love. Instead of seeing the broken scared girl I felt inside, I saw a confident determined woman smiling back at me.

I think adrenalin got me through the event. It was as if I was watching from afar as I greeted Ian's friends from university, whom we hadn't seen for many years, and reminisced with them and then went over to say hello to his work colleagues. Once everyone had left and I returned home, I was so worn out by the day's proceedings that I went straight to bed and, mercifully, fell into a deep restful sleep.

"Dear Ian, I'm exhausted. I feel as if you're close to me tonight. Perhaps it's because I'm on my own for the first night since you died. I know you are watching over me. Good night, my angel."

Ian's family suggested that a portion of Ian's ashes were scattered at Parkview, where Ian was born. I agreed and went along to see his mum and dad disperse the vestiges around a flowerbed carefully prepared by Pat, a keen gardener. I knew having her son's remains at home brought great comfort to her.

A few days after our intimate and emotional gathering, Pat went into the garden to find a yellow balloon resting among the shrubs there. Like me, yellow was her favourite colour, so she knew this was a sign from her beloved son.

I didn't feel ready to scatter the rest of Ian's ashes until a few months later, but when the right time arrived, I knew exactly where to take them. Very early one morning, just as the sun was rising, I drove a few miles from our home, and scattered his remains in the woodland there, close to a bridle path where Ian and I had enjoyed many a canter on Moose and Willow and where I had seen bluebells dancing in the dappled sunlight of springtime.

Yet again, my spirited husband had the last laugh. Having emptied the contents of the urn, I returned to my car and drove into town to buy a large coffee. As I walked through the door of the café, a flash of grey caught my eye. I shook my head and smiled. There, on the toe of my shoe, was a smattering of Ian's ashes.

Even in the saddest of times there is humour to be found.

Scattering his remains had given me some closure on the sad events. Now I needed to rebuild my life, a life alone. Determined to make Ian proud, I promised to fulfil my dreams in his memory.

My granddad, Harry, and me on Blackpool beach, 1972

Me aboard Pendleside SnipSnap, before he galloped off with me

Always the student: writing and horses have been a common theme from an early age

Ian astride his mum's horse, Guinea

Ian and I mountain biking in the Lake District on our first holiday together, 1991

Enjoying time together in France, 1997

Ian and I messing about at home while on hols from university

Willow and I enjoying the fresh air

Ian and his beloved Moose

Ian and Moose tackling the cross-country course at Hambleden Horse Trials

And in action, training over an enormous fence!

Ian and Moose at Gatcombe horse trials in 2006

The hardwork pays off. Ian receiving his rosette from HRH Princess Anne at Gatcombe Horse Trials

Team White with Australian eventrider, Bill Levett.

Photo courtesy of Fiona Scott-Maxwell

Willow and I training February 2007

Photo courtesy of Fiona Scott-Maxwell

Ian enjoying the local produce in Sorrento 2007; our last summer holiday

Wilbur and I flying

Handsome Wilbur

Wilbur and I winning rosettes in dressage

Moose and I enjoying a cuddle in 2010

Harry joins the clan

Mole arrives – what a cutie!

Angel signs: one of the many hearts that have turned up

The first Ian White Memorial Trophy awarded in 2009

Beautiful Baz brings joy to my world.

Photo courtesy of Fiona Scott-Maxwell

Chapter 17
A mother's love

"*D*ear Ian, my mum is staying with me. We have had such a lovely time together. Quality time with Mum is something good that's come out of all this shit. We sorted out your probate together. Goodness, it felt so final. Too final. That A4 piece of paper told me I was your widow. Your widow? What does that mean? I'm your wife, dead or alive. I will always be your wife. No-one else can take you. I'm yours forever."

I wouldn't have made it through those months after Ian's death without the incredible support of my friends, family and work colleagues. Some people, whom I remain great friends with today, came into my life after Ian's death, either because they were widowed themselves or because they empathised with my situation despite never having experienced it. And many shared my passion for horses.

One person who stood by me like a rock was my mum. She looked after me as only a mother can do. Receiving her unwavering care and love was particularly special because Mum and I haven't always been so close.

As a child, I was a tomboy. Clothes were for comfort rather than fashion and dresses were not conducive to playing football with the boys at school or being in muddy paddocks with horses. When I did relent and wear one of my dresses, I stubbornly insisted on wearing my trainers. She once called me 'plain Jane' because I rarely wore make-up. I'm certain it wasn't said with malice, but it stuck with me. I don't think she fully understood my enthusiasm for being outdoors, in the countryside, or my apparent lack of interest in men. She often called me a 'women's libber' and I wondered if my fiercely independent streak scared her or perhaps she envied my freedom, being of a generation who married young?

On reflection, I think my desire to stand on my own two feet, unwilling to accept help, pushed her away. However, that all changed when Ian died. For the first time in my life I felt extremely vulnerable. I had no energy left to put up any resistance to well-meaning support. My barriers, those barricades we erect for self-protection, were well and truly smashed to pieces. Goodness, I needed my mum more than anyone and, of course, she came to my rescue.

We spent many a weekend together following Ian's death and shared some lovely mother-daughter moments.

Mum came with me to shows to watch me compete, often standing in the freezing cold or horizontal rain to cheer me on, always on hand to muck in as required. She loved riding in the horsebox, too.

"Oooh, aren't we high up? I can see over everyone's garden walls," she exclaimed on her first journey.

Although Mum had never been around horses or had her own pets, my animals adored her for her calm and gentle demeanour.

In early May 2010, we enjoyed a day out at Badminton International Horse Trials, a first for Mum. The size of the cross-country fences blew her mind and I struggled to keep up with her as she popped in and out of the many trade stands with their varied merchandise. I certainly know who I get the love of coffee and cake from.

These were all fun outings, but what I loved most was having the chance to really get to know my mum and see how emotionally intelligent she is. Despite never having shared the same loss, she could somehow relate to my situation and empathise. I had always seen her as a quiet and shy person, but when it was just the two of us her true personality shone through and I enjoyed experiencing this side of her. We are in tune with one another about life, the Universe and spirituality, too. I received little tokens of her love through the post, including crystal angels and cards containing beautiful words, so I knew she was thinking of me even when we weren't together. These small but significant gestures had a huge impact on me and I will forever treasure those special moments I had with my mum.

I will never forget the kindness of Ian's mum, Pat, either, who treated me like a daughter. Though we had supported each other throughout Ian's illness, his death brought new challenges. Our emotions were very raw and, as time passed and the adrenalin subsided, I felt I needed time apart to deal with my own grief.

During one particular visit to their home, Pat and I were talking about Ian and she was describing events from his childhood. The memories cut deep and her voice trembled and faltered as the pain of remembrance became too much to bear. I moved to put my arms around her, to comfort her, but inside my head I was screaming out, "What about me? You still have your husband to share your grief. I want to remember Ian as my husband, not as your son."

I felt ashamed and selfish because of my apparent lack of empathy, but I knew I needed space for a few months: distance to grieve for my husband, not a son or brother. I know this was tough for Pat because she told me so a few years later when sufficient time had passed for us to enjoy each other's company again.

Despite these difficult times, my recovery and personal growth didn't go unnoticed by Pat. During a visit to see my in-laws about three years later, Pat and I were chatting in the kitchen while stacking the dishwasher. I was telling her about my plans and what I'd been up to.

"Kathryn, what I love the most is watching you blossom as a person in your own right," she said. "That takes courage and I am so proud of you."

Her words meant a lot to me given she was still grieving for her son. I think it's testament to the strength of our relationship that we could be honest with each other.

Pat has now joined her son and I miss her company. We had a very close bond and I feel blessed to have had such a fabulous woman as my mother-in-law, with whom I shared the very best and worst of times

Part Three

Picking Up the Pieces

Chapter 18
The aftermath

"*D*ear Ian, today I stared at my phone, at your name, in disbelief, willing you to ring me, to hear your voice. Why? Why are you dead? Why you? I can't get it straight in my head at all. Life is shit. I am fed up with trying to be cheerful and positive all the time. I want you back. I keep remembering those times in hospital when we were so full of hope yet so fearful of the diagnosis."

I found the strength to face the months after Ian's death from feeling his 'presence' very closely around me.

I busied myself with tasks. I couldn't bear sitting alone in the house with my thoughts. Images of him lying in the hospital bed or collapsing due to a seizure or, the worst, him lying on his death bed permeated my imagination if I sat still for any length of time. I couldn't focus on anything for long, either. My attention span was shot. Reading even a short email was impossible. Four words in and I'd lose track of what the sentence, let alone the email, was about.

The content of my favourite TV programmes suddenly seemed trivial, too.

Although Ian and I had lived in this house for the past six years now I was newly widowed I felt insecure in my own home.

I had lived on my own before, when I first moved away from Nottingham and rented a bedsit, but this felt different. Back then I still had Ian on the end of the phone. Now it felt as if I had no-one to make sure I came home safely from a night out or look after me when I was ill.

I put padlocks on the gates to my garden and attached security chains and additional bolts to the front and back doors – and I would check they were locked, two or three times, before going to bed.

While being at home alone was difficult enough, going out into the real world was even more challenging. All around me people laughed and joked, getting on with their lives, seemingly without a care. Meanwhile, my world was tumbling into a deep dark hideous abyss.

Occasionally, I'd be caught off guard. A song would play on the radio or I'd see a couple walking hand in hand, something that would remind me of Ian.

"I'm a widow now. Me. A widow. My husband is dead. He's never coming back."

The words would spin round and round in my mind, taunting me, goading me to cry, to break down and weep. And that gut-wrenching pain, deep in my stomach, would be back. I was in denial. I know that now. My coping strategy was to not acknowledge the tragedy that had happened. It all felt far too surreal to be true.

"Dear Ian, the end of another week. I used to love Fridays. The thought of coming home to you and going to the pub where we would excitedly plan our weekend and tell each other about our day. Now Fridays are just another evening tinged with sadness. I miss you, Ian. I miss you so much."

I remember coming back from a meeting in West London. As I sat on the train watching the scenery whizz past the window, my mind wandered to the time when Ian missed his last train home after a night out with his work colleagues.

I was in bed when the phone rang, jolting me awake. Blinking furiously, I tried to focus on the alarm clock beside the bed. One in the morning. I reached out to the bedside cabinet and grabbed the phone. Ian.

Nervous laughter.

"Ri-i-i-ght," I replied slowly, as I realised where this was going.

"I'm not sure, not sure when the next train is...."

I sighed. "Where are you?"

He slurred the name of the train station. Clearly worse for wear, and on his own, he was unsafe. Despite my reservations about driving in central London, I had no option. I had to rescue him.

"Stay where you are," I instructed sternly. "I'll be with you in about 30 minutes."

"Thank you. Thank you, my lovely. I love you."

"Hmmm, just stay where you are, OK?"

Rubbing my eyes sleepily, I dragged myself out from the warmth of the duvet. After pulling on some jogging bottoms and a sweatshirt and wiggling my feet into freezing cold plimsolls, I headed out into the pitch dark to the car.

Mercifully, the roads were quiet and I soon approached Marylebone station. The traffic lights ahead of me turned red so I quickly rang Ian's mobile. It diverted straight to voicemail – but not to his, to his friend Dave's. I still, to this day, do not know how he had managed to do that.

The lights changed and, throwing the phone onto the passenger seat, I followed the road round to the left, scanning the pavements either side for a familiar figure. Nothing. Another set of lights brought me to a halt again so I tried ringing my husband once more, but Dave's voice sang out, bright and cheerful, telling me, rather unhelpfully, that he wasn't available to take my call.

"Where the bloody hell are you?" I exclaimed out loud, trying to suppress the panic rising within me at the thought of driving round central London, unable to find Ian.

Turning left, I approached the first junction for the second time and something caught my attention. Someone was hunched over the railings by the pelican crossing.

I pulled over and unlocked the passenger door.

"Get in," I hissed, keeping one eye on the traffic in front of me.

Ian looked up and I saw the relief flooding his pasty white features. He launched himself over the barrier with renewed vigour now his lift had arrived.

"Thank you," he whispered, sheepishly, as he settled into the seat beside me.

I grunted in response, easing the car forward.

"I'm really grateful," he continued as he got himself comfortable. Five minutes later he was asleep with his mouth open; gentle snores reverberated round the car. I shook my head and rolled my eyes. Thank goodness I'd found him.

A couple of weeks later he went out again, with strict instructions ringing in his ears NOT to miss his train. Later that same evening, around 11.30 pm, he rang.

"Please tell me you are on your way home," I said before he had a chance to say hello.

"I am," he replied but I noted a hesitation in his tone.

"But," I said.

"Er, but I fell asleep and missed my station so I'm now heading towards Leighton Buzzard."

"Oh, for God's sake!" I couldn't help but laugh at his predicament and neither could he.

Needless to say, he caught a taxi home, but he never lived those two incidents down.

∞ ∞ ∞

"*Dear Ian, almost a year since you left, and how my life has changed. I miss you dreadfully. Sometimes I just sit in stunned silence, contemplating all that has happened.*"

During those first 12 months after Ian's death, I now realise I was fuelled by adrenalin. Nothing I would ever experience in life would be that painful; nothing I faced in the future would be that bad. His illness and passing put everyday problems into perspective. 'What do I have to lose?' became my mantra, which enabled me to confidently tackle challenges I faced during that period. I also felt enveloped by his love,

However, the simplest of things could still bring me to my knees in despair, like the first clothes wash I did. I loaded up the washing machine and one of Ian's t-shirts fell to the floor. I picked it up and buried my face in its soft, comforting material, inhaling deeply, desperate to internalise the smell of my husband. I felt like I was washing him away, out of my life forever.

"Dear Ian, today was tough. I feel as if I'm wiping you off the face of this earth by taking your name off all the household bills. It's not right. I can't believe you're never coming back. I want you here so badly."

Cleaning the house, I felt as if I was removing his presence from our home; wiping away any remnants of his existence.

I even missed tripping over the abandoned pile of clothes on the bedroom floor and hitting my shins on the open drawers he'd left open – stuff that infuriated me when he was alive. I cleared out some items of Ian's clothing, but decided to keep a few things to wear myself, like his socks and one or two of his sweatshirts. Yes, the jumpers were too big for me, but who was going to see me snuggled up in those in the evening? I punched extra holes in his leather belts and I still wear those to this day.

I bagged up the remaining clothes and donated them to charity. Seeing them hanging in the wardrobe was too painful. I felt that giving them to the local charity shop was Ian's chance to make a contribution – fundraising was something he'd said he was going to do if he survived. A terminal illness certainly makes you acutely aware of the amazing work these organisations do.

"Dear Ian, I threw out some of your clothes today. I never knew you had so many pairs of underpants!"

Photos became very important to me. I created a book containing pictures of me and Ian competing our horses and gave them to my family and in-laws. I spent one Sunday afternoon hammering nails into the walls around the house so I could hang up photos depicting treasured memories of our life together.

I was frightened of losing these memories, of them fading away over time.

I even had a life-sized canvas made up of the photo of Ian and Moose taken at Gatcombe horse trials after his presentation with Princess Anne. Many times, I have stood in front of that photo and 'talked' to Ian or just cried. These pictures and mementos gave me great comfort during the darkest hours.

I listened to his voice on our answerphone. Over and over again I'd play that message.

Thank goodness for all the video footage of our eventing fun, too. Seeing him. Hearing him. Anything to try and keep him alive in my mind.

"Dear Ian, I can't believe we are hurtling towards the one-year anniversary of your death. Where does time go? Reaching this milestone seems to confirm that you're never coming back, but I don't think I truly believe, or accept, that I'll never see you again. It's all

very surreal and the pain is still raw. I miss you dreadfully. I can't sleep tonight so I'm staring out of the bedroom window. The moon is beautiful — I think it's a new moon. Very bright and perfectly round. It's lighting up some of the surrounding clouds. I know you are out there somewhere. I keep hoping you'll appear in our garden. Stay with me forever."

Chapter 19
Team White minus one

Once more, horses provided me a lifeline. Willow and Moose were now all that remained of my and Ian's family unit, of Team White. I threw myself into looking after and riding them in a desperate attempt to divert my attention and remain occupied.

Eventing still appealed to me so I decided to compete Moose in Ian's honour. My friends thought I was crazy because of his size and strength, but I trusted him. And I trusted fate. I no longer feared death. I know this sounds reckless and selfish, but what did I have left to lose? My life partner, the man I was meant to grow old with, had gone. Horses and eventing provided a strong connection with my married life, and so they continued to be my focus and provided a great distraction from the horror of the previous six months.

"Dear Ian, I'm no longer frightened of dying. In fact, dying young and being with you is less frightening than living another 30 years without you."

I planned to compete Moose at a one-day event in August and entered Willow for an event in July.

Though I no longer feared my own mortality, I became increasingly worried about either of my horses becoming injured or having to be put down. They not only held a strong connection to Ian, but they kept me busy – I didn't want to have time to let my thoughts wander.

"Dear Ian, tomorrow is my first event with Willow and I know you will be there with me. I am excited because eventing is our passion, isn't it? And I'm sad because I can't share this day with you."

The day of my first event with Willow dawned bright and cheerful, matching my optimistic mood. Being out and about again felt great, though there was a bittersweet tinge to everything now that I was competing alone. Often, when I climbed into the cab, I would see the empty passenger seat and cry.

After an hour on the road I turned into the driveway of the venue. Horseboxes lined one side, and on the other were the show jumping arena and shopping area. Behind those the cross-country course stretched out into the distance.

My heart pounded with excitement on hearing the commentary, ringing loud and clear across the countryside. I was back out on the eventing circuit, with a horse whom I trusted, and I felt more determined than ever to make the day a success.

While Willow happily munched on her hay net in the lorry I grabbed a coffee and made my way over to the cross-country start box to walk the course.

"Bloody hell, Kathryn, what have you done?" I thought as I walked from one fence to another.

During my absence from the sport the fences appeared to have grown, seeming much wider and taller than I remembered. Thank goodness, I had been sensible and entered a lower level class than usual. I shook my head to clear my doubts. Willow and I were both more than capable of getting round clear; I just needed to concentrate and be confident.

Clearly pleased to be out again, Willow performed a beautiful dressage test which the judge scored highly. She followed this with a clear round in the show jumping. Now it was all down to surviving across the country to be in with a chance of winning a rosette.

For the cross-country phase, each rider provides a brief paragraph about themselves, their horse and any eventing achievements, which the commentator reads out while you gallop over the fences. The piece I wrote for that day came from the heart and the words flowed easily. I explained I was competing in memory of my late husband, Ian. The commentator, whom I knew, came over to me afterwards to say that my bio had given her the biggest challenge of her career. Keeping her emotions in check as she read what I had written had been difficult; she knew the words were so heartfelt.

Willow and I jumped those cross-country fences without a glitch and I wore the biggest grin on my face as we crossed the finish line. I was thrilled with our performance and so proud of Willow.

"If she doesn't stop patting that horse's neck, she won't have a neck left," joked the commentator.

We were rewarded with a sixth place so I attended the prize-giving. This was when the realisation hit me. I was on my own. No Ian. No in-laws. Just me. I received my rosette to polite applause from my fellow competitors and bit my lip to fight back the emotions bubbling up inside. It was a poignant ending to a glorious day.

Having survived my first competition without Ian, I now needed to focus on preparing Moose for our debut appearance together. I took him cross-country training a couple of times to get used to riding him over solid fences and he was an absolute gent. I was beginning to feel much more confident about my decision to compete him.

Then disaster struck.

During a sedate hack around the nearby woodland Moose suddenly became lame and the lameness remained after several days. I withdrew our entry from the impending competition and called out the vet. Moose's welfare was paramount and I took this setback as a sign that I wasn't destined to compete him. After all, he was Ian's horse and perhaps this was Mr White's way of letting me know he was still his.

"Dear Ian, Moose now appears to be lame. I will look after him, my darling. He's with me for the rest of his life. I wasn't meant to compete him, he was your horse. I swear his injury has happened because he misses you. You were such a team – my two gorgeous boys."

The vet examined Moose and diagnosed ligament damage. Treatment with ultrasound was prescribed, followed by a period of rest before starting a strict exercise regime. Moose became rideable again after a few months of in-hand work, but I was advised never to jump him.

By now I was back working full time. I would ride one horse at 5.30 am before work and then ride the second after commuting back from the office. I enjoyed being busy, but this punishing schedule was tiring. In addition, Moose was becoming increasingly nervous around traffic and I'd had a couple of close incidents with cars due to him spooking into the road.

I related my concerns to a friend, Annabel, over a cup of tea.

Ian and I became acquainted with Annabel through eventing because we often hired her all-weather gallops and cross-country course to train. She would always come over and say hello to us if we were competing at the same events, and we cheered Annabel around her first ride over the enormous Badminton International cross-country course in 2005.

"Why are you still riding him?" she asked. "Is it because you feel an obligation to Ian or is it to keep that part of your life alive?"

They were good questions. Moose didn't need to be ridden. He didn't owe me anything. He'd given Ian so much joy. If he couldn't jump and he was becoming less predictable to hack, all we had left was dressage. And he hated dressage. What was I trying to achieve? Who was I doing this all for?

"You're right. I'm going to retire him."

I'm pleased to say he took to retirement very well and relished being out at grass 24/7. With only one horse to exercise I had more time to concentrate on Willow's training. However, Moose's sudden and unexpected lameness made me paranoid about Willow becoming injured or ill. What would I do without my horses to ride? Riding was my escape, my reason for getting up in a morning. Something needed to be done, and fast, because I was no longer enjoying my one and only pastime.

"Dear Ian, it is Sunday morning. I miss you. I miss our life together. Last night, I watched videos of us eventing. I didn't cry this time. In fact, I felt comforted watching you in action. I feel so much love towards you. Maybe the video footage makes me believe you're still here. Goodness, a lump has come into my throat now. Even two years on, I still struggle with being on my own and sitting still – I'm scared of silence so always have the radio or TV on in the background. I'm trying very hard to slow down and not be constantly busy; I'm exhausted."

Chapter 20

Tapping my way to happiness

"*D*ear Ian, I knew these months were going to be tough, but I didn't realise just how vividly I would remember certain moments of your illness. It's as if I'm transported back in time, reliving the excruciating fear and the pungent clinical smell of the hospital ward."

My worries about injuring Willow impacted my confidence, but I couldn't bear the thought of not riding so I sought help and serendipity lent a hand.

Jo, a coach specialising in helping riders with confidence issues, had contacted Janie at the online eventing magazine to discuss some articles she was writing. Spotting an opportunity and knowing my concerns, Janie put me in touch with Jo. Her specialty is a technique called TFT (Thought Field Therapy), a form of acupressure which involves tapping traditional acupuncture points with your fingers to release physical and emotional complaints.

It was worth a try.

Due to the physical distance between us I had my first session with Jo via telephone. It lasted for two hours, during which I sobbed like a baby and felt drained afterwards, but goodness, did it have a positive impact on my riding.

"I want you to give me a number between one and 10 for how worried you are about riding Willow, with one being very worried and 10 being not worried at all," she explained.

"Three," I replied, giving her the first number that came into my head.

"OK, I want you to follow my instructions. I'm going to ask you to tap different points on your body using the middle finger of one hand. You will tap each point about five times."

This I did, tapping specific points on my head, face, collarbone and hand, guided by Jo. I followed this sequence a few times before saying aloud, "I can do this, I will do this."

Then I would either repeat the tapping sequence or rate how I felt between one and 10. Each time, I said the first number that came into my head.

Despite my open mind I had concerns that I would be the one person for whom this technique didn't work. So imagine my surprise – and relief – when the numbers in my head genuinely started to increase as the session progressed.

In between the tapping sequences we discussed recent events that had led me to contact Jo. I began to understand that my feelings were perfectly normal after experiencing such a tragic and significant life event. Fear of losing my ability to ride Willow was perfectly understandable. Horses represented a large part of who I was and how I spent my time. Without Willow to ride I faced a very different life to the one I knew and loved. I also feared losing another member of our family.

"Dear Ian, I spoke with Jo this evening. With her guidance, I went through the images of when you were ill and now I can imagine them with less trauma. I feel the closeness we shared instead."

By the end of our meeting my rating had increased from three out of 10 to eight. And that's not all. That night I slept the best I had in months, having released deeply suppressed emotions.

The real impact, however, was the significant difference I felt when riding Willow. My renewed confidence shone at competitions, too. Following that single session with Jo, Willow and I went out and won three competitions, back to back.

"Dear Ian, I know that you were with me today because Willow won! I don't know why I'm telling you this because I'm sure you already know. A strange thing happened in the show jumping arena. The wind suddenly became stronger as I was halfway round the course. I felt like I was in a bubble of calm and I was talking and laughing with you. I must have momentarily zoned out. It was extraordinary – but it worked – we jumped clear.

"Winning was bittersweet because you weren't there to give me a hug or enjoy the day with me. I am determined to keep going, though. I will make you very proud of me, Moose and Willow. We are still Team White, with you, our guardian angel, our chef d'équipe in spirit!"

Our victories qualified us for dressage championships, where we were placed in the top 10.

I still use this tapping technique, not only when I compete, but also when I need a boost in self-confidence at work or in my personal life.

Chapter 21
Letting go

"*D*ear Ian, I finished repairing the shed roof tonight. I know it's a bodge job, but at least it's now more waterproof than it was. It felt good to be out in our garden, but I desperately wanted to come indoors and find you, to put the kettle on and have a cup of tea together. The house feels quiet and empty."

Ian's death certainly helped to put stuff into perspective.

When Ian was alive I would never have contemplated carrying out house maintenance or DIY – this was very much Ian's domain and I wouldn't have known where to start on most things. In fact, I know I would have worried so much about doing the wrong thing I wouldn't have even started. Now I asked myself what the worst outcome was, and could I live with it? And, often, the answer was 'Yes'.

Perhaps I was driven by a need to prove to myself that I was independent and capable of living on my own – and surviving.

Selling my car was one such task. Ian's car was the newer of the two so I placed an advert in the rear window of mine. I didn't have to wait long for an enquiry. A couple of days later a potential buyer phoned while I was in town shopping. He'd seen the advert while shopping.

"Can I come round to take a proper look at the vehicle?" he asked.

He offered to meet me by the car and follow me back home. That was when alarm bells rang in my head. A feeling of vulnerability, of being alone, flooded my senses. But I needed to sell the car. What was I to do?

A flash of inspiration – an idea – popped into my head.

"Yes, OK," I replied. "I'll be five minutes."

Sure enough, a young man stood by my car. I arranged for him to follow me so he could see it driven and inspect it.

Only I didn't go home.

Before heading to the carpark I rang John at the stables and explained my predicament. We agreed that if I drove the car to the yard he would wait for me and help with the car sale. The sale was a success and I patted myself on the back for my innovative quick thinking.

Unfortunately, not long after, Ian's car became unreliable.

Some mornings, it had taken two or three attempts to start the engine and this worried me. What if I had to drive at night and I broke down? Sensibly, I was a member of a breakdown service, but the fact there was no longer anyone at home to check I was safe, to look out for me, made me anxious.

I decided to change the battery to see if this resolved the issue. I'd watched Ian do it before; it wasn't that difficult.

I was due to meet a friend for coffee, but given the damn car wouldn't start yet again I had no option. I had to change the battery there and then. Fortunately, I had already purchased one for this very moment, but just hadn't got round to fitting it. Of course, it wasn't a bright dry day, so there I was, under the bonnet, muttering expletives as the rain poured down the back of my neck.

"Typical. Just bloody typical," I swore as I grappled with the spanner, trying to undo the stubborn nuts holding the square plastic box in place.

The spanner kept slipping round the bolt and I couldn't see a smaller one in the toolbox. Feeling utterly defeated, there was nothing else I could do but ask for help. Not something I'm good at.

The lights were on in my neighbours' house so I scurried up their driveway and knocked on the door. They were a married couple whom I spoke to on a regular basis and I had even had coffee with her once or twice, but, interestingly, I hadn't seen them since Ian had died. Through the small panes of glass in the kitchen window I saw the husband emerge from their lounge. I swear a look of panic crossed his face as he saw who was calling.

"Don't be so ridiculous and paranoid," I told myself sternly, forcing a smile on my face while he grappled with the lock.

He opened the door just enough that he could speak through the crack.

"Of course," I thought. "His wife isn't home. I'm now a single woman. I'm widowed, so I'm clearly desperate for male company and he's worried I'm going to..."

My thoughts tailed off as he said hello and asked if I was OK. I sighed. Perhaps I was being unfair, though he clearly wasn't going to invite me inside. My clothes were soaked, my hands black with oil. My patience was fast running out. I brandished the spanner at him that I was still gripping and felt rather pleased when a look of alarm crossed his face. I quickly explained my situation through gritted teeth. He shook his head.

"I'm sorry, I can't help you," he responded, without moving.

"Right, OK, well thank you," I stuttered, "I'm sure I've got one somewhere that'll fit."

He closed the door as I turned to return to the car, feeling somewhat dejected by his attitude. Thankfully, this was the only time my new status as widow caused any problems with people I knew. Some people just don't know how to react to bereavement and, if I'm honest, perhaps I hadn't either before death had come calling so close to home.

I took a deep breath and phoned my friend to explain the situation. Unlike my neighbour, she came to my aid. Within minutes, she arrived to take me into town to buy a suitable spanner. Battery changed as well as clothes, we had coffee and cake to celebrate.

"Dear Ian, the heartache is relentless, and not helped by the fact I'm tired and irritable. I'm tired of hitting brick walls and tired of my own company. Your car is being a right pain in the neck, the washing machine needs replacing and my tax bill has to be paid. I know I need to pull myself together. Feeling very alone right now."

A few weeks later, and accompanied by my mum, I traded the car in for a newer model and negotiated with confidence.

As the salesman scurried off yet again to discuss my requests with his manager, my mum leaned over to me and whispered, "Darling, are you sure you need new mats and road tax?"

"Absolutely," I whispered back, smirking. "Look and learn."

I was enjoying myself. Not only did he agree to include shiny new mats and a year's worth of road tax, he threw in a full tank of petrol too. I think mum was a tiny bit proud of her independent 'women's libber' of a daughter and gave me a big hug when we got home.

"You were brilliant in there," she said. "You're doing great."

∞ ∞ ∞

"Dear Ian, Christmas fills me with dread. On the one hand, I can't wait to see the back of 2008 because it's been the worst year of my life; on the other, I don't want to leave 2008 because I feel as if I'm leaving you behind."

The hardest part of that year was the first Christmas without Ian. Of course, I knew it was going to be tough. Ian's family had invited me to theirs for the day, but as the big occasion got closer I knew I couldn't be with them – I wanted to be in my own home. As fate would have it, a close friend of mine was also on her own that year so we arranged to meet up at the stables where she kept her horses.

We had a delicious cup of coffee there, followed by lunch at her house and a cheeky glass of bubbles, surrounded by her little posse of dogs. A simple day spent with a great mate, and it remains one of my best Christmases ever.

Over the following 12 months, there were a lot of 'remembrance dates' and firsts. Days when I'd think back to what Ian and I had been doing the previous year or the first wedding anniversary without him, his birthday, my birthday. They went on and on.

"Dear Ian. Bloody hell – dates! This time a year ago, you were in the John Radcliffe. You were trying very hard to persuade the doctor to let you come home. We were on such a high driving home, weren't we?"

That first year also taught me an important life lesson that I practise now daily. When you open your heart and mind to opportunities and are clear about what you want, the Universe delivers, albeit in its own timeframe.

Fate, if you prefer, has played a huge role in how I met many of the lovely friends who have come into my life since being widowed. In particular, I find the company of other widows to be invaluable because we truly understood what each other is going through. I didn't feel the need to be a part of a formal widows' group – though I know there are several wonderful organisations which provide invaluable support online and face-to-face – as it happened, I didn't need to be because I met these incredible women purely through serendipity.

For example, a work colleague of mine dropped into a local bookstore one Saturday. It just so happened that a book signing was taking place that day. The author, Sheila, lived in the next town to mine and her book described how she had rebuilt her life after being widowed a year earlier. My colleague gifted me the book.

Reading her story, I realised how much Sheila and I had in common so I emailed her to let her know how much her book had helped me. The rest is history. We became firm friends, bonded by a shared experience, and helped each other through the ups and downs of widowhood for several years afterwards.

I met another wonderful widow while organising Ian's funeral. I asked our friends and families to donate to a couple of charities in Ian's memory, one of which was World Horse Welfare, a cause close to my and Ian's hearts. I emailed a request for donation envelopes and explained my situation. I received the most beautiful response from one of the team there, Jean, who recounted her own story and offered her support, for which I will always be grateful.

We became penpals, sharing our thoughts on widowhood, horses and life in general via email. On Ian's birthday I donated money to buy a tribute tree in his memory and a couple of years later we met in person when I travelled to Norfolk, to the World Horse Welfare Hall Farm, to see the sapling I had sponsored.

This wonderful scheme enables those bereaved to remember loved ones, human and animal, or important events by sponsoring one of the beautiful trees planted alongside the paddocks, which provide shelter and protection to the recovering horses who graze there under this charity's care. A plaque is placed beside each specimen, inscribed with a personal message from the sponsor. Jean and I now meet every year for a natter and a catch-up over lunch – a close friendship born out of grief.

Another acquaintance happened even before Ian became ill, via my job as clinical researcher.

Jim was a physician based at a hospital in Manchester, one of the sites I managed as part of an ongoing clinical trial. I visited him and his team every three months to monitor their progress and review their data. Despite his busy schedule, Jim, a personable chap, always had time for a chat over coffee, and it would appear we had a common interest – writing.

They say everyone has a book within them," he said, as he stirred sugar into his coffee.

"Oh yes, they do," I nodded. "I'd love to write a novel one day."

"Me too," he replied. "I'll let you know when I've started mine."

Interesting how certain conversations, simple exchanges, stick in your mind.

About two months later, Jim was signed off work. He had noticed blood in his stools and terminal bowel cancer was confirmed. Despite not knowing him that well, I was shocked by the suddenness of the diagnosis and saddened when I received an email from his team to let me know he had passed away a few weeks later.

After Ian died, I felt compelled to contact Maria, Jim's wife, to share with her the conversation I had had with her husband about writing a book and to offer her my support as a fellow widow. Having never met her or even spoken to her, I was rather relieved, and delighted, when she replied to my email. We kept in touch for a year or two, sharing anecdotes and experiences. We eventually lost contact as our lives moved on though I understand one of their sons has now followed in his father's footsteps and become a doctor.

A shared experience and tragedy can bring people into your life, even if it is only for a short period. Over the years, other wonderful women, all bereaved of their husbands, have become friends and acquaintances, with many of us sharing a passion for horses and a love of the countryside.

Not only that, but my social circle has widened generally as I've slowly rebuilt my life. Since Ian's death, I have made a conscious effort to go out and socialise. I haven't hidden away. My love of horses has proven a great avenue for meeting people through having a mutual interest.

"Dear Ian, this weekend was a lot of fun. I enjoyed having friends to stay. It felt lovely to have our cottage filled with laughter again. This used to be such a cheerful place – our haven. I enjoyed cooking and looking after everyone.

I do confess to having a private weep in the kitchen, though, so as not to make a scene.

"Thank goodness for my friends. I wouldn't have got this far without them. Sitting on the fence watching Moose graze yesterday, I was feeling particularly low.

I wished I could have ended my life there and then – if I knew we would definitely be together again. But I'm still here because I know you wouldn't want that for me."

Chapter 22
Angel whispers

"*Good bless you Ian, you were too special for this world and heaven has gained a very special angel – your star will shine bright. Kathryn, my dearest friend, you will always have your own very special guardian angel who will always be with you.*"

Tribute from a close friend.

The overwhelming love I felt from Ian, on a spiritual level, was so strong that I received what I believe to be signs from him. Some may argue they're coincidences, brought about by my desperation and grief, but, given their impeccable timing and relevance to me or my situation, I like to think they are angel whispers. And, most importantly, they provided comfort.

Although I am a scientist and deal with data and logic on a daily basis, I do believe there is some form of life after death. Or, at least, I can rationalise the existence of a person's energy after they have passed. After all, from a scientific perspective Newton's third law of physics states that energy is neither created nor destroyed; it can only be changed from one form to another. Given we are all, as humans, made up of energy, where can that all go when we die?

I didn't have to wait long for the first sign to arrive as one appeared just 24 hours after he passed away.

The year before Ian's illness I attended a training course, organised by my employers, who, I have to say, were incredibly forward thinking and innovative in their choice of workshop topics. An external speaker from the US, who worked with top athletes, described how we can radically improve the way we live by changing our 'life story', the stories we tell ourselves based on past experiences and beliefs.

I remember being completely absorbed by his own stories of how he and his team had helped professional sportsmen and sportswomen overcome mental hurdles to achieve their goals and win medals. I came away inspired and bought the book he recommended, called 'Chasing Daylight'. Authored by Eugene O'Kelly, the CEO of a large corporation, KPMG, the book describes how Eugene lived the last three and a half months of his life after terminal cancer was confirmed.

The story was positive, despite the ending, and was a beautifully written reminder of how we should embrace our lives and the time we have with loved ones.

I passed the book on to Ian after writing inside the front cover, 'Dear Ian, don't forget to keep following your dreams, all my love always, Kathryn xx'. He read it on what was to be our last summer holiday together, in Sorrento, and was also moved by the uplifting story. We kept the book, but thought no more about it.

Two days after I returned home from the hospice this book popped into my mind and I felt compelled to read it again. I scanned the first few pages, feeling like someone else was guiding me to a particular point in the story. Sure enough, at the place where Eugene is diagnosed, my mouth fell open. I had completely forgotten that Eugene had brain cancer – and exactly the same type of tumour as Ian.

That wasn't all. As I continued to flick through the book a note fluttered out onto my knee. On it was a handwritten message.

I smiled as I read what Ian had written.

'Manage energy not time; focus on the perfect moment; live for now; circle of friends; spontaneity – perfect often seems to go hand in hand with unscheduled; change your thoughts and you change your world; by gliding along you do the world and yourself no favours; you can always push a little harder, be a little braver.'

They were prompts clearly made for himself – learnings he'd made from reading the book, but at that moment, as I read his list, I felt as if his words had been put there for me to find, to guide me as I started this new chapter in my life without him physically by my side.

I have placed this note inside a photo album I created for Ian's 40th birthday: a smart pale brown leather book in which I collated photos of Moose to tell his story from the day we met him to action shots of him and Ian clearing fences at Gatcombe. I added a narrative, as if Moose was talking. Ian loved it. I have since added printed copies of the kind messages of condolences I received from his friends, colleagues and family and now this note lies beside them.

Another angel gift was the arrival of my cat in October 2008. Annabel's mum accompanied me to the local rescue centre. A cat lover herself and a widow, she was keen for me to have some company at home. She knew first-hand how lonely life could get when you are suddenly thrown into a life of involuntary singledom. Although I was more of a dog person, I knew that, given I would be returning to work at some point, I needed a house pet that better fitted in with my lifestyle.

We walked along the rows of glass cages looking at the cats of all different ages, sizes and colours. The choice was overwhelming. A little ginger kitten, with a twinkle of mischief in his eye, came running over to the front of his enclosure, eager to say hello. For a moment I was tempted, but then a vision of him swinging from my curtains and sitting in a cloud of feathers from the sofa cushions came to mind. We walked on.

All the other cats were reserved; that is, until we came to the last enclosure.

Here a handsome grey-striped tabby attracted my attention as he strutted up and down the front of the cage, clearly wanting a stroke. I pushed my hand through the little round hole in the door and he immediately pressed his soft fur against it, purring. I looked at the ticket stuck in the corner and gasped.

"Oh, goodness, look, he's called Oliver."

This was the same name as Annabel's cat. He hadn't been reserved, either. This was a sign. I felt sure.

"He's the one," I said, turning to Rosie.

"Are you sure?" she asked.

I nodded.

"Shall we go and find someone to see if we can take him?"

I nodded again, but added, "I'll stay here. I don't want anyone else to have him."

I was that sure he was mine.

Rosie returned with a member of staff, who unlocked the cage door. As soon as it opened Oliver jumped out.

"He wants to come home now," Rosie laughed.

A fortnight later I collected this little furry bundle, who meowed all the way home from the confines of his carrier. I renamed him Harry after my maternal granddad, with whom I shared my love of horses. I felt he suited this name better than Oliver.

Slowly, over the next few weeks, we built the beginnings of a strong bond. This 'tough little street cat' became a purring sofa companion and his trust in me increased. The first time I took him to the vets for his annual check-up he growled as soon as he came out of his carry crate onto the examination table and scanned the room for possible escape routes. The vet, seemingly unaware of his increasing anger, continued to chat away to her colleague while dispensing his vaccination injection.

"Sorry, could we inject him quickly?" I asked, gingerly holding the enraged tiger in my arms. "Only I don't think I have long before I get clawed."

On his second visit, a year later, I prised him out of his crate once more, but this time he immediately pressed his little furry body against me. Though concerned, he clearly had more trust in me and didn't growl once.

So what other signs have I received?

Well, the first was during the church service when Ian's death was announced. My close friend Maggie, who came to stay with me frequently during that first year despite living over two hours away, came with me.

Maggie and I had met through our love of horses when I answered an advert she'd posted in a local riding magazine. I had just moved to Buckinghamshire and she was looking for a sharer for her horse, Mistie. I was desperate to ride again after my time at university. We met and I instantly fell in love with Mistie. Best of all, Maggie and I got on really well, too. We have been great mates ever since and I will be forever grateful for Maggie's compassion during Ian's illness and since.

So off we went to church that Sunday morning, just a short walk through the village from my home. The sun was out and, though cold, it was a beautiful start to the day.

We entered through the large arched doorway and settled into a pew towards the back. Sat beside me, Maggie put her arm through mine and gave it a companionable squeeze. I smiled and looked up at the window to my right. Rays of sunlight were streaming through, making the dust in the air sparkle and dance with its warmth and energy. I closed my eyes and took a deep breath.

Despite being unfamiliar with the service, both of us managed to keep up with the proceedings and even enjoyed the opportunity to have a good sing along.

Then the time came for the declarations of marriages, deaths and births.

The vicar moved forwards to address the congregation and cleared his throat as he unfolded a piece of paper containing the announcements. Was it me or had the light in the church dimmed? I looked around me. The beautiful sunny beams were being blocked by the clouds, rendering the stained-glass windows less sparkly and dull. Marriages and births done, the vicar rustled his paper and adjusted his glasses. As he did so, rain began to hammer on the windows. I shuddered and pulled my coat more firmly around me as the temperature suddenly dropped.

"Ian White," the vicar began, but his voice was drowned as a loud rumble of thunder crashed overhead, following a bright flash of lightening that lit up the altar.

More lightening and a smaller clap of thunder followed, then silence. A few seconds later, and bright sunny beams poured once more into the nave, bathing us all in ethereal light.

Maggie and I looked at each other in utter amazement.

"Well, that was dramatic. Well done, Ian," she whispered, grinning.

"Dear Ian, yesterday a large crow flew down our chimney into the front room. I had to crawl on my hands and knees to open the front door to let that the damn bird out and avoid being hit by its frantically flapping wings. Not funny, Mr White!"

On several occasions I thought I saw Ian. If I was out and about, I'd see the back of someone's head and for a split second I'd think it was him before disappointment drowned my hope. However, one night I had a vision in which I saw him clearly.

Mum had gone home that day and I lay in bed feeling very alone, listening to the comforting tic-toc of my alarm clock on the bedside table, willing sleep to come and stop my mind from whirring over recent events. Then I felt the bed move. It shook as if someone was trying to grab my attention. My eyes flew open and there he was. Ian was standing by the side of my bed. Surrounded by green-yellow light, he gazed down at me.

"Oh, Ian!"

I desperately wanted to reach out and touch him, but I felt paralysed.

"Please put your arms around me and tell me this has all been a terrible dream," I thought, staring in disbelief at what I saw.

He looked so real, but then he began floating away, up towards the skylight. Once more I tried to move my arms, to grab hold of his hand.

"Please stay."

The voice in my head was small, desperate, pleading.

Frustratingly, I remained motionless, unable to move, and watched as this vision faded away. The familiar hurt returned deep within me. I curled up into a tight ball, pulling the duvet up over my head, and sobbed for my loss. What I would have given for one more second of being with him, one more time to hold each other, to tell him I loved him.

"Dear Ian, thank you for visiting me last night. It was so real. You had yellow light all around you. I wish you hadn't had to go. You floated off – faded. Please visit again. I will never ever tire of your visits. As I write this and look at the photos of us, I can't believe you've gone. It still hurts so much."

I experienced something similar a few nights later when I woke up – or at least I think I woke up – to what felt like someone getting into bed beside me. I froze. Frightened. Alone. What was happening? Had someone broken in? Instinctively, I reached out my arm to his side of the bed and felt the warmth sear through my body as Ian, it had to be Ian, wrapped his arms around me. He held me close and I felt safe, reassured. I concede that these night-time 'visits' were probably the figments of my despairing mind, but I cherished them for the comfort they gave.

There have been more tangible signs, too.

I arranged to visit Ian's work colleagues at their offices to say hello and return his laptop. I was familiar with his office so I decided to get there early to catch up on my own work in the library before meeting his co-workers for a coffee in the atrium.

As the time of our get-together neared, I became increasingly emotional. Handing over his laptop felt like losing another piece of him. Biting my tongue to stop myself from crying, I stood up and gathered my belongings together. I would pop to the women's loos to wash my face and regain my composure before heading for the café.

Thankfully, the bathroom was empty and I chose, at random, a cubicle to go into. I turned to close the door behind me and something shiny on the floor caught my attention. I gasped. Right by my feet was a sparkling silver foil heart. You know the type you see in card shops as confetti? I bent down to take a closer look and picked it up in my hand. I knew right away this was a sign from Ian. He was with me. Of all the cubicles to pick, I had picked the right one. The tears flowed untapped as I slipped the precious heart into my pocket. So much for composing myself. I dabbed my eyes dry with a tissue, took a deep breath and made my way into the hustle and bustle of the foyer, reassured that my guardian angel was right there beside me.

More hearts have appeared over the years in all sorts of different places: around the house, in the garden, in the car. They always turn up when I am in need of reassurance.

One year, I re-visited Tilley Farm, located in rural Wiltshire, a magical place where I can leave any stress at the gate and completely relax. I attend workshops here for a training method called Tellington Touch (TTouch), a gentle technique I use with my horses and other animals.

I have Ian to thank for finding this wonderful place. A keen researcher, Ian had been looking for ideas to help him with Moose, who fidgeted a lot when tied up. He came across TTouch and, in typical Ian style, he booked us both on to a one-day workshop, which opened our eyes and minds to this incredible training method. Keen to learn more, we enrolled onto a week-long training course and took Moose and Willow with us. Ian was the only man there among 20 women, which demonstrates how in touch he was with the gentler side of life – more than I had appreciated when he was alive.

We both fell under the spell of this beautiful location, where we met some wonderful people, some of whom remain friends today. I can honestly say we had the best holiday because we, and our horses, were so relaxed. I joked that Willow would have lit scented candles and played soothing healing music in her stable there.

A year after Ian's death, I visited Tilley Farm again, firstly because I totally believe in the power of TTouch and secondly because here was a place where I felt comfortable to go on holiday alone and be with like-minded people.

Driving through the gate, I instantly felt relaxed and I felt Ian's presence very strongly indeed. I gathered with my workshop colleagues in the large airy classroom, catching up over a coffee until we sat down for the course to begin. I opened my notebook, one I had randomly chosen from my collection at home, and couldn't believe my eyes when, there on the page in front of me, lay a silver foil heart.

Ian could also communicate with me via the radio.

One Sunday morning, I drove over to my sister-in-law's house for a family birthday party. It was a month after Ian had died and I felt apprehensive about the occasion. These family gatherings stirred up so much raw emotion and grief.

I got into the car and said quietly to myself, "Ian, please let me know you're with me. I need you beside me today."

I switched on Radio 2 and sang along to the upbeat tunes as I drove. Half an hour later, I was close to my destination.

Once again, I asked for his help and said aloud, "Ian, please give me the strength to get through today."

I couldn't believe it when the music suddenly became distorted.

"Ian, is that you?" I thought. "No, no, don't be silly Kathryn. The signal must be a bit weak here."

I continued up the winding hill, thinking the signal would become stronger again at the top.

The crackling became louder as I reached the summit, followed by complete silence. Then, to my utter disbelief, a haunting organ melody began to play. The interruption lasted only a few seconds before more spluttering and gurgling and my usual radio station returned. I smiled. I knew this was a sign from Ian letting me know he was with me. I took the same route home later that day and no such interference occurred on the way back.

Ian's pièce de resistance happened on our wedding anniversary, our first since his death. Understandably, I awoke feeling low and tearful. I needed an 'Ian fix' so I decided to watch our wedding video. A family friend had filmed our special day and, after watching it a couple of times, we had filed it away to gather dust. I knew it was in the house somewhere, but could I find it? Emotions ran high as I stomped up and down the stairs, getting increasingly exasperated.

"I know it's you. I know you're hiding it from me," I shouted out loud. "I am going to watch this damn video, so just show me where it is, Ian. Stop protecting me."

Drawers were opened and slammed shut and Harry the cat ran for cover.

Then a thought struck me: what if it had been where I thought it would be – in the DVD drawer under the TV, of course – but had slipped down the back and out of sight?

Genius! There it was. I grinned.

"You see, I told you I was going to watch it."

And I did, blinking through a whole stream of fresh tears.

The video ended and I stood up to switch off the television. Out of the corner of my eye something outside caught my attention. My mouth opened with astonishment. I rubbed my eyes, not believing what I saw was real. There, in a tree at the bottom of our garden, were two balloons, their flight curtailed by their satin ribbon streamers entangled in the branches: one was lilac; the other was ivory. The colour scheme of our wedding. I suspect they had escaped from a party held at the neighbouring pub; regardless, I knew from the colours and the timing of their appearance that they were a message to me from my special guardian angel. I photographed them on my phone and texted the picture to a friend as a reality check. She confirmed she could see them, too.

"Dear Ian, it is our ninth wedding anniversary and I never thought we'd be spending it apart. You are, however, a clever, lovely man. I know it's you who put those balloons in the tree opposite our house. I know because only you would know to have one ivory and one lilac and just as I had finished watching our wedding day DVD. Your speech that day was beautiful – understated and sincere – you to a tee. We were so in love. We were so right for one another. You should not have had to leave so early, but the world – my world – was and still is a much better place for having had you in it."

The next morning I looked out of the window to see if they were still there. Could I have dreamed it all? No, they were there alright, but deflated and wrinkled. I wish I'd taken them out of the tree to keep. Why didn't I? Maybe they weren't for anyone's possession. Interestingly, I lost the photo when my phone broke a week later. Clearly, they were there for me to see on that one day and that one day only so I understood their significance.

The following year, I received another sign on our anniversary, though this one wasn't as romantic, as this entry in my diary reveals.

"Dear Ian, er, thanks for my anniversary present – not quite what I expected. Janie said I was being a little greedy asking for a flypast by the Red Arrows. She told me I should look out for banana skins. Clearly she knows you better than I do because two days after my request I dropped like a stone to the ground, having slipped on a rotten potato skin that must have fallen out of a neighbour's compost bin. I now have a bruised knee to remind me of you!"

Chapter 23
Tragedy strikes twice

I took about a month off work after Ian's death before gradually phasing back. I know this doesn't sound very long, but I felt isolated and lonely at home. I needed to be busy to escape my thoughts. In the office, I had company and my projects kept my mind occupied.

Six months later, I was working full-time again when a second tragic event knocked me back off my feet.

I visited the North Norfolk coast with Janie, owner of the online eventing magazine. We travelled there with our horses and stayed a couple of nights. A cold and bitter November wind blew and grey skies threatened heavy rain. We stabled the horses at a farm within riding distance of the beach. Although they offered bed and breakfast within the cosy interior of the farmhouse, we decided to camp in Janie's horsebox, which had a living area with beds and a hob – but no heating.

Despite the wintry conditions the place was idyllic, with a village pub a short walk away where they served delicious food in front of a roaring open fire. Furthermore, we could ride to stunning Holkham beach along an extensive network of bridle paths that bordered open stubble fields and meandered through pretty ancient woodland.

We arrived late afternoon and settled our horses into their new surroundings. The stables were located within a large airy barn. The stalls were separated by a wooden partition with vertical metal bars about shoulder height, which the horses could look through. Considering the pair had never met before Willow and Jimmy got on very well and frequently stood side by side in close companionship over the weekend.

The next morning dawned bright and sunny, but with a cold winter nip in the air: perfect conditions for a gallop along the sand. We set off on what was an hour-long ride, enjoying the feeling of freedom as we cantered along set-asides around the arable farmland leading us to the coast.

Despite the long trek, our horses' energy levels soared the minute their hooves touched the sand and the vibrant salty smell of the sea hit their nostrils. We jig-jogged down to the water, Janie and I laughing at their antics.

Holkham beach is a popular place for horse riders due to the wide expanse of sandy shore, which is flanked by a soaring pine forest on one side and the blue-green choppy North Sea on the other.

Above us sea gulls cheered us on as we walked along a stretch of the beach where we then planned to canter back towards our start point. This enabled us to locate and avoid any soft patches when we were going at a faster pace, thus preventing an injury to our horses' legs.

"Shall we?" Janie turned to me, grinning.

"Yes, let's do it," I laughed back, turning Willow to line up beside Jimmy.

We counted to three, pressed our heels into our horses' sides and leant forward in our saddles, allowing our steeds to surge forwards. Whoosh! Off we went, the wind whistling around us.

"Woohoooo!" I screamed, squeezing Willow's sides with my legs, urging her to go faster.

Jimmy and Janie kept up beside us and I swear I could see a huge grin on Jimmy's face. His ears were pricked, as were Willow's. I felt alive. I felt Ian with me. Tears streamed down my face due to the stinging cold sea air and the emotional release from this exhilarating feeling of freedom. For those few minutes I forgot all my worries and angst. I felt liberated. This was a childhood dream come true and a thrilling experience I'll never, ever forget.

We neared the end of our track and stood up in our stirrups, keeping our weight further back, to encourage the horses to slow down. Both of them could have gone further.

We slowed to a walk, our horses' sides pushing our legs out and back as they took deep breaths to recover from their efforts. Their blood was up and Willow was clearly keen to jog all the way back home. It took all my concentration, and the calmness of dear old Jimmy, to persuade her to walk. I patted her neck, damp with sweat and hot with exertion. I looked across at Janie who, like me, was disappearing into a cloud of steam rising from our horses' bodies.

What glorious, adrenalin-fuelled fun.

Back at the farm we made sure the horses were dried off and comfortable before heading to the horsebox to open a bottle of red wine. Every so often we would look out of the little window to see our beautiful ponies munching happily on their hay.

The wind was picking up and, as we sat watching DVDs of Badminton and Burghley horse trials from years gone by, rain began to pelt against the metal bodywork. We pulled duvets tightly around us, thankful for our shelter, as the vehicle began to sway.

"How strong do you think the wind has to be to knock this lorry over?" I asked Janie, drowsily; the alcohol was taking effect.

"I think we'll be OK," she responded, her eyelids drooping

The gentle rocking and the soporific wine eased us both to sleep that afternoon and I'm sure I relived that morning's beach gallop in my dreams.

"Dear Ian, my trip to Norfolk was out of this world. Janie was great company, though I wished you had been with us. I dreamed about you both nights so I know you were there in spirit. I find it comforting when you appear in my dreams. They are so vivid – your touch, your smile, they're so real. I just feel so sad when I wake up and remember the painful truth. But please keep visiting, my clever angel."

Our weekend excursion came to an end far too soon. Once more I faced the prospect of returning to an empty quiet house, the worst aspect of time away from home. Turning the key in my front door and making my way through a silent house was awful. Oh, how I longed for Ian to be sitting on the sofa watching TV, to welcome me back so that I could share my experiences with him.

Worse was to come.

Three days after returning from Norfolk, I awoke to the shrill sound of my phone ringing. It was John from the stables.

"Kathryn, you need to come up to the yard. It's Willow. She's not right."

The urgency in his voice stirred me out of bed instantly. This was serious. John was a skilled horseman, with many years of experience, who could deal with most injuries and problems. It wasn't yet 7.30 am and the vet was already on his way.

I arrived to find John in Willow's stable. Her head lowered and her sides damp with sweat, she looked distressed. She repeatedly turned to look at her stomach, tell-tale symptoms of colic, a painful condition affecting the horse's gut. My dear horse was clearly in a lot of discomfort.

John handed me the rope attached to her headcollar.

"Don't let her roll," he instructed. "Keep her walking until the vet arrives. I'm going to the top of the driveway to see where he is."

The theory is that if horses roll during a colic attack they can twist their gut, which can prove fatal.

I stroked her nose and laid my forehead on hers. Closing my eyes, I took a deep breath, inhaling the exquisite scent of horse.

"Don't leave me," I sobbed. "Sweetheart, it's not time, it's not time for you to join Ian. We have so much yet to do. Please, please don't die."

I don't know how long I stood there with my eyes closed, but when I opened them and looked round John was standing at the door, his eyes moist with tears.

"She's going to be OK," he tried to reassure me, but his face, etched with concern, gave his real feelings away.

The vet came three times over the course of that morning, but Willow's condition was deteriorating so he referred her to the Royal Vet College, a half-hour drive away. After helping me load Willow into the horsebox John offered to come with me, but I declined his kind gesture. I was getting used to dealing with stuff on my own and I wanted to be with Willow for as long as it took without feeling any pressure to come home.

The veterinary team was waiting for me as I jumped from the driver's cab.

"Unload her and bring her round to the main doorway," the head vet explained, pointing to the examination area.

Slowly, Willow and I made our way across the tarmac to a large barn, inside which were computer monitors and veterinary equipment of all shapes and guises. After conducting a thorough examination, the head vet turned to me.

"She's going to need surgery so that we can get a better idea of what is causing her problems. There's no point you hanging around here. We'll call you as soon as we have more answers."

Reluctantly, I handed the lead rope over to her and gave Willow's velvety muzzle a kiss.

"Keep strong, beautiful girl," I murmured before walking out, thankful that she was in such great hands.

Hearing my return, John and his wife came out to greet me as I parked up.

"This is turning into a very shitty year," I muttered, my teeth gritted, eyes stinging with tears. I stared at the ground, unable to look at either of them in case I broke down.

John's wife put her arm around my shoulders and steered me to their kitchen where she gave me a steaming cup of hot sweet tea.

"I think you should go to your friend's house like you planned," she said gently. "There's nothing you can do here. Willow is being well cared for and I don't think you should be alone tonight."

She was right. I rang my best friend Anna, explained the situation and, having packed an overnight bag, started my journey north.

Halfway up the A1, my phone rang and I pulled over. It was the head vet.

"Willow is currently in theatre and I'm afraid it's not great news."

My heart sank.

She described the problem and Willow's prognosis. While surgery was possible, the recovery period was lengthy, during which Willow would be stabled and on medication. I asked the vet to give me five minutes to consider if I wanted them to bring her round from the anaesthetic. I rang John.

"If she was mine, I'd let her go," was the advice and I concurred.

I wanted Willow to have quality of life; to be a horse. Spending the next six months in a stable, with little if any time out in the field while receiving a cocktail of drugs wasn't acceptable in my opinion. I called the vet back.

"Let her go."

My voice, cracked with emotion, was barely audible.

When I hung up, the bright digits on the dashboard of my car caught my attention. The time of that phone call was 5.40 pm. The day was 15th November – six months to the time and day of Ian's death.

I sat in that layby, with the wind and rain battering my car, and howled, beating my fists on the steering wheel in utter desperation. How bloody unfair could life get?

"Dear Ian, what the hell is going on? Poor, poor Willow. I hope you are reunited. If you are, make sure you have fun together and please give her lots of cuddles. I will miss her so very much. She was my best mate and confidante. I'm struggling to understand why my horse has been taken – why Willow?

"I trust you, Ian. I know you wouldn't intentionally hurt me. A voice in my head suggests you're actually looking after me – Willow was 13 years old, her age making her more prone to injury and illness. Perhaps you don't want me saddled with two retired horses – is that it? What do you have planned, my lovely? Please don't leave me without a horse to ride and compete. This is what I do. I need to ride to survive."

I somehow made it to Anna's. She opened the door to be greeted by a puffy-eyed mess. My head thumped from dehydration. I hadn't eaten or drunk much since breakfast that morning. My fantastic friend had cooked a delicious dinner, which I couldn't face. In fact, I curled up on her sofa after taking some painkillers and fell asleep. Great mate I wasn't, but she was and I will always be grateful for the kindness she showed me that night and ever since.

When I returned to the stables the following morning, I walked down to Moose's field. Normally, he ignored me if he was grazing. Grass came before other such pleasantries in Moose's world. This morning, however, was a little different.

As usual, he was out of sight, but as I stood there and called his name I heard the unmistakable beat of hooves on turf. Up the hill flew Moose, chestnut mane and tail streaming out as he galloped towards me. I stood still. Something inside me told me to stay where I was despite half a tonne of horse approaching me at speed. Sure enough, he skidded to a halt just in front of me, pushed his soft muzzle towards me and blew warm air onto my hands. I'm certain he knew; he knew that Willow had passed on. I stroked his beautiful face with that distinctive white blaze. He let out a deep exhalation and we stood quietly together, remembering our dear friend.

Willow's passing was meant to be. I see that now. It unleashed all the anguish and despair I had suppressed deep down inside of me to survive these past few months, to endure life after Ian's death. Losing her emptied the last remaining reserves of my strength. I saw my GP and asked to be signed off work until further notice, to finally give myself some time to grieve and recover.

With Willow gone and Moose retired, John kindly offered me rides on his horses. Every day, he and his team rode out for morning exercise, around the lanes and leafy tracks that crisscrossed our village. I joined them, glad to be in the fresh air, to have a purpose, a reason to get out of bed. I cherished this fantastic opportunity to ride a variety of horses of all sizes and ages. John and his family took brilliant care of me and I remember those days fondly.

Riding John's horses gave me the motivation I needed to look for one of my own again. I didn't have to wait long, either. As I've said earlier, I truly believe animals find you, and so it was with Wilbur.

Chapter 24
A Valentine's surprise

January 2009, and a couple of months after losing Willow a friend told me about a horse who was for sale. "He's called Wilbur," she explained. "He's five years old so the perfect age for you to take on his training."

"Great name," I smiled. "I like the fact it starts W-i-l, like Willow."

I arranged to go along and meet him.

I arrived at the yard where he was stabled and grabbed the bag containing my riding hat from the boot of my car. I smiled when a pair of riding gloves dropped to the floor which I thought I had lost a few weeks before. I was getting used to these 'signs' and I was sure this was a good omen.

Wilbur was stunning. His glossy dark brown coat with faint dapples was punctuated by three white socks and black mane and tail. A white strip of hair, about two inches wide, ran the length of his face between kind eyes that exuded wisdom beyond his years. He was beautifully put together, everything in perfect proportion, from his graceful arched neck to his rounded powerful hindquarters.

The positive vibes continued when I sat on his back, and I instantly knew he was right for me. He gave me a great feeling under saddle and I adored him. All my lofty ambitions of eventing at higher levels of competition went out the window. At that moment I didn't care if we only jumped a twig. I knew this horse and I were going to have fun together.

Would you believe it? Wilbur came home on St Valentine's Day 2009, a poignant date for me because Ian had made a promise to me the year before. We spent Valentine's Day 2008 in the ward at Stoke Mandeville hospital. "I hope you're going to do better than this next year," I joked.

"Oh, I will, don't you worry," was Ian's response.

Despite his physical absence, he stayed true to his word because I know in my heart he sent Wilbur.

"Dear Ian, thank you for a very special Valentine's present. Wilbur is fantastic. I already love him. He's a great distraction."

Part Four

New Beginnings

Chapter 25
Flying solo

"*D*ear Ian, I know how I want to live the rest of my life, however long I may have. I want to live as if I have only today to be alive. To cherish the present and not take life for granted. To be strong, stand up for my beliefs and not be afraid to have my own opinion. To give something back to society. To see the best in people. To follow my instinct and my dreams. To be a ray of sunshine and to continue to make you proud.*"

May 2009, and I felt it was time to return to work. Wilbur's arrival had given me a new focus and Moose was enjoying retirement. Slowly, my life was returning to some semblance of normality, albeit significantly different to how it had been. The rest of the world was getting on with living and Ian's death was now 'old news'. I needed to get back into the swing of things myself and craved the company of my colleagues, not to mention the distraction and brain stimulation. I loved my job and had brilliant and supportive co-workers. I wanted to go back.

One of the most significant lessons I'd learned following Ian's death was that the Universe (or fate, if you prefer) delivers whatever you want in life, providing you truly believe in it and are specific about what you want. Then you open your mind to the opportunities presented to you. Once more, serendipity lent a hand in unfolding my future when a colleague emailed me a couple of weeks before I was due to start phasing back.

"A secondment opportunity has come up in the medical writing department. I know how much you enjoy writing in your current role. Are you interested? I'd be happy to put your name forward if you are."

In my role as clinical researcher I had gained valuable experience of creating and editing documents using the data generated from the clinical trials I managed. This documentation is submitted to regulators who can approve or reject the launch of a new medicine based on this information. It is a critical part of developing new treatments and the aspect of my job that I loved the most.

If I moved into medical writing, then producing these documents would become my fulltime occupation. I had always dreamt of becoming a writer and here was my chance to make a living from wordsmithing.

I didn't even have to move companies, which was a relief. I didn't feel mentally capable of making such a big change at that time. I had a successful interview and, at the end of the six-month trial period, became a permanent member of the medical writing team. Unbeknownst to me then, this was going to be a life-changing move.

Two years on from Ian's demise and I was finding the daily commute to the office more challenging. Not only were the roads becoming busier, I missed being at home. During my time off I'd met more people from my village and widened my local social circle. Being in the office every day I felt cut off from home life and my community.

Surely there was more to living than this daily routine?

The great feedback I received from my project teams and colleagues made me feel confident about the prospect of going freelance.

A few years before Ian's diagnosis, I pondered the idea of self-employment, but given he was already contracting and we had significant financial commitments, a mortgage and two horses to support, the sensible option was for me to remain in employment.

Now, however, I was viewing the prospect of running my own business with a changed perspective after experiencing such a significant and life-changing event. Inevitably, the loss of a loved one makes you query everything about your life.

One question kept spinning around in my head as if it was taunting me: 'If you were diagnosed with a terminal illness tomorrow, what would you wish you had done in your life? What would be the life of your dreams?'

Nothing would ever be as bad as watching Ian die so what did I have to lose by freelancing? One of my favourite quotes is 'Leap and the net will appear'. Well, plenty of others had made the leap and survived so why couldn't I?

Greater autonomy and the challenge of managing my own business really appealed. More than anything I wanted to honour Ian by following my heart and my dreams, something he never had the chance to do.

I knew deep down I was making the right decision, but the change felt huge. I wanted someone to hold my hand through the transition so enlisted the help of a life coach. This was my future and I wanted to make sure that, however long I had left on this earth, I had truly given it my best shot.

Chapter 26
Writing my future

You know what? Once I had made the decision to go freelance I didn't have to wait long to find a brilliant life coach. Synchronicity was working for me yet again.

One Monday morning, a colleague and I were catching up with our weekend exploits.

"Oh, I've just remembered," said Lisa, busily rummaging in her bag. "I saw this in the paper and immediately thought of you."

She handed me a newspaper cutting containing a book review for 'The Blue Skies of Autumn: A Journey from Loss to Life and Finding a Way Out of Grief', written by Elizabeth Turner.

"Thank you," I replied, turning it over to read the back cover.

I ordered a copy that day.

Elizabeth's husband had been killed in the 9/11 terrorist attack in New York City. There on business, he was attending a meeting in the World Trade Center when the planes struck the buildings. She gave a beautifully written and honest account of her recovery following this tragic loss, made particularly poignant by the fact that she was pregnant with their first child.

I found her book uplifting and devoured every page, comparing and contrasting my life with hers and taking great comfort from her story. Here was a young widow, like me, who had successfully rebuilt her life. Not only that, but having time off to grieve allowed her to re-evaluate what was important to her and she subsequently changed career from HR consultant for a TV company to self-employed life coach.

If anyone could understand my situation and help me get my life back on track, it would be this lady. I emailed her and relayed my own story. She sent a lovely response and referred me to her business partner and fellow life coach, Kevin.

"I'm taking a break from coaching individuals," she explained.

A week later, I nervously prepared myself for my first session, to be conducted via Skype at 8 pm, not knowing what to expect. I needn't have worried. Kevin immediately put me at ease with his relaxed style of coaching. I recounted my recent past while he listened. And he *really* listened because he recapped what I'd said, adding his interpretation and asking thought-provoking and relevant questions. I felt reassured. I knew he totally understood me and my situation.

One thing stood out for him. Given all I had been through I still thought I could plan the future. I like to be in control and become anxious if I don't have a strategy in place.

"You of all people," he said softly, "given what you have recently experienced, must realise that life isn't like that."

Change is inevitable. Just when you think you have life sorted, fate throws a curve ball that takes you in a completely different direction. Through my coaching with Kevin, I practised the art of 'going with the flow', becoming more attuned to, and congruent with, the Universe. However, it's an ongoing process. When things get tough, I revert to my default behaviour as planner, but the difference is I now recognise when I'm doing it.

I'll never forget the feeling of euphoria I had at the end of that call. I'm not an evening person at all, but, despite the late hour, my energy levels were bursting through the roof. For the first time in months, I genuinely felt an overwhelming enthusiasm for life and optimism about the future. I barely slept a wink that night thanks to the adrenalin coursing through my body yet I awoke the next morning feeling revived and refreshed like I'd slept soundly all night. A wonderful calmness followed. I now knew I had to trust in the Universe and let my intuition guide me forwards to live a more fulfilling life.

The first step was to become self-employed so that I could finally spend more time at home and realise my ambition of becoming a professional writer.

With Kevin's continued support and encouragement, I resigned from full-time employment in July 2010 and became the proud business owner and director of Cathean Ltd, a company offering medical writing and equestrian journalism services.

Later that year, synchronicity played its part again when I met business coach Elaine. She was the keynote speaker at the first medical writing conference I attended. She gave a presentation on how to work more efficiently and had a similar style to Kevin. I liked what she had to say and was intrigued to find out more so when I returned home I contacted her.

She coached me for the next five years, during which she helped me to develop my business and gave me the confidence to organise my own annual workshops for fellow freelance medical writers, which I still do today. I love meeting up with my freelance colleagues and I have formed great friendships along the way. Not only that, but I have presented seminars and have written articles to share what I have learned from working with Elaine and Kevin.

I think it was coaching with Kevin that ignited my interest in spirituality and the power of the Universe. He helped me to understand how magical things happen in your life when you identify and let go of your limiting beliefs – the stuff that holds you back. Trusting in the Universe and my intuition has taken me down paths I would never have previously considered possible, including being a writer and business owner. The Universe always has the bigger picture in mind so when things don't turn out as you expected, don't worry. The Universe has your back and all will work out in the end.

Follow your heart, strive to do what you're passionate about and you'll always succeed.

Chapter 27
Can you love again?

J ust as I was embarking on my new business challenge, my personal life took a surprising twist. They say you find love when you least expect it. Well, in August 2010, I met someone even though I wasn't consciously looking. Honestly, the thought of being back on the dating scene at the age of 37 filled me with dread. Luckily, I'm happy in my own company so the thought of being single didn't faze me. After all, I'd lost my soulmate, who was irreplaceable, so a widowed spinster I would remain – though others had different ideas.

During a visit to see my parents, only a few months after I was widowed, we went along to the annual arts and crafts fair in the village where they live. I had loved attending this event as a child so relished the opportunity to return. The only issue was that it was held in the church where Ian and I had wed. Well, I was going to have to get used to revisiting places we'd been to as a couple – I could either avoid or face them, and I chose the latter.

Taking a deep breath, I pushed through the doors into the church hall, where several tables were set up displaying local artists' products. I sauntered round the room admiring pottery and paintings and enjoyed chatting with friends of my mum and dad whom I hadn't seen for a while. The vicar who had married Ian and me came over to say hello and gave his condolences. He then uttered the words I had heard several times over the past few weeks and, quite frankly, hated hearing.

"You're so young, I'm sure you'll find someone else in the near future – don't let the opportunity to love again pass you by."

Irritation crackled in my throat and before I had chance to catch them, the words had already escaped from my mouth.

"I have absolutely no desire to meet anyone else, thank you. There's nothing wrong with being single. I shall be a happy spinster for the rest of my life."

I fixed him with a steely glare, my chin jutting forward determinedly, challenging him to dismiss my response. Anger burned inside of me. I was mad as hell.

"Oh yes, yes, of course," he stuttered before nodding his acknowledgement of someone else he needed to speak to over the other side of the room and disappearing as quickly as he had appeared.

Tears were pricking my eyes, threatening to give away my feeling of disappointment and sadness. I turned to face the pictures exhibited behind me, and then I saw it. A quotation written in beautiful calligraphy, bordered by a gold-coloured frame:

"To the world you are just one person, but to one person you are the world."

"Oh crap!" I thought as the tears spilled over and gave me away.

Thankfully, my mum was close by and, sensing her daughter was in need, she came over and put her arms around me and consoled me. Needless to say, those framed words came home with me and sit on my bedside table.

Having resigned myself to being on my own for the rest of my life, I wasn't expecting to meet anyone, but, yet again, the Universe knew best and had different ideas.

James and I already knew of each other through our shared equine connections. We had met once before at a luncheon organised by a mutual friend, who, unbeknownst to us at the time, was trying her best to match make. Nothing happened on that occasion, but a few months later James and I were helping out at an equestrian event. This same friend ensured James had my phone number and instructed him to 'look after me'. I was slowly integrating back into the eventing community and volunteering at events like this was a great way of giving something back to the sport and getting out of the house.

I spent two days there. James came over to say hello at the start of the first day, during the officials' briefing. Text messages followed. By the second day, the exchanges were becoming more flirtatious. At the end of the final day, he came over to me to say goodbye and I felt something had shifted between us. There was a definite spark; something more than friendship simmered beneath our farewell. So it didn't surprise me when he got in touch with me a few days later and the flirting continued for a few weeks via email until he suggested we met up.

He was travelling to an event not too far from my home. The plan was that he'd stay over at mine before heading off to another event in the region.

Having tentatively agreed to his suggestion, I found all the angst we face as teenagers came flooding back, but it seemed ten times worse. I had been with the same man for the last 18 years. What if I was really rubbish at kissing and Ian had just been polite about my lack of skill over the years? As for sleeping with another man – oh, goodness! Alcohol. I would definitely need copious amounts of liquor to calm the nerves. Having been fortunate never to have had any concerns about my body in the past, here I was, hurtling towards 40, with more hang-ups than a telephone.

I won't lie: that first kiss with James felt very odd, and it felt appropriate that we slept in the spare bedroom rather than the bed I had shared with Ian. I tried not to make comparisons between James and Ian, but it was inevitable given it was early days and I was still grieving. Looking back, I never really let go of Ian in my head or my heart. There were three of us in that relationship, however well James and I got on, and perhaps that was indicative that this liaison was always going to be transitional.

"Dear Ian, did you send James to me? It seems as if you did because it doesn't feel wrong to feel this way about a man again. I feel your presence as strong as always. Keep looking after me – please don't ever leave my side."

Being with Ian had opened my heart to love and I think this gave me the confidence to court romance again following his demise. Early on in our relationship, Ian questioned my motives for being with him.

"Do you really like me?" he quizzed. "Only you don't give a lot away."

The truth was, I liked him more than I had ever experienced liking anyone before, but internally I was battling my insecurities: Why did he like me? Why wasn't he with the pretty blonde who had thrown her arms around him on the dance floor that night Ian and I had first kissed? I felt as if my heart was encased, shielded from potential heartbreak and hurt. Priding myself on being a strong, independent woman, I wasn't comfortable with letting my guard down and showing my softer side. Yet over the years Ian and I were together, my trust grew and I found the courage to peel away the protective layers and surrender to my true feelings and love for Ian.

With the benefit of hindsight, however, I see how vulnerable and desperate for physical contact I was. Several of my friends thought it was too soon for me to be with another man and I know Ian's parents struggled with the idea of me being with someone else. They wished me happiness, but made it clear from the start that they didn't want to meet James. I respected their viewpoint, but I was disappointed by their attitude. They had each other and I wasn't going to turn down the opportunity to be in a couple again and find happiness.

James provided love in abundance and, furthermore, he seemed happy to talk about Ian. He was the perfect partner for me at that time and over the five years we were together he helped my recovery during the toughest time of my life.

He brought out the fun side of me and we laughed a lot. He loved music and reading song lyrics, as did I. We sang along to the radio whenever we went out in the car together; it had infuriated Ian when I karaoke'd from the passenger seat. He was laid-back and lived life at a much slower pace than me. Being with him made me realise how my frenetic pace of life added to my stress levels. Keeping busy was my defence mechanism, blocking my thoughts about the tragic events of my recent past.

One story highlights this beautifully.

James came to stay for the weekend and arrived to find me up a ladder in my bedroom, trying to fix an errant smoke alarm which kept going off at random times of the day and night. The batteries needed replacing. Anger bubbled up within me as I struggled to unlock the protective cover and access the battery compartment. My arms ached from straining to reach the sodding alarm and stabbing, painful spasms shot through my neck.

"Can I help?" he asked.

"I can't get this bloody cover off," I grumbled while glaring at the ceiling. "I just can't do it." My voice trembled as I fought back the urge to have a full-blown tantrum. "I can't do it," I growled again. "These things never used to happen when Ian was alive."

I wrenched at the stubborn device with my fingers, splitting my fingernails as I grappled with the plastic cover, which remained resolutely in place.

James gently placed his hand on my leg.

"Come down," he cajoled. "Come down and I'll help you."

His voice, calm and reassuring, encouraged me to make my way down the stepladder. He wrapped his arms around me as I howled and sobbed into his chest, releasing pent-up frustration.

"Where do you store your screwdrivers?" he asked, gently wiping my tears away with his thumb.

Off he went downstairs to retrieve the tools he needed while I sat on the bed, glowering at the circular plastic device that taunted me from its lofty position above the stairs.

"Right," he said on his return. "Take this and lever the cover off just there," pointing out a specific spot on the cover with the screwdriver.

James was no fool. He knew that replacing the batteries himself would make me feel like I'd failed so he talked me through the process, step by step.

The batteries successfully changed, I climbed down from the stepladder once more, my legs leaden. Months of grieving and staying strong were taking their toll.

"You OK?" asked James, a look of concern in his eyes.

I nodded.

"Right, stay here for me – sit down on the bed."

He patted the crumpled duvet before disappearing downstairs again. A few minutes later, he returned with the largest gin and tonic I had ever seen.

"Drink this," he commanded, sitting down beside me.

I did as I was told, gratefully gulping the contents down. Glass drained, he carefully took it from my hand and wrapped his arms around me once more. I surrendered into the warmth of his body, feeling protected.

"Promise me," he said gently, "that you will please, *please*, slow down. You can't continue to live life like this."

"Dear Ian, things are still going well with James. I love him dearly. He has the patience of a saint. He needs it being with me – an emotional wreck of a woman. Is that why you sent him? I haven't laughed this much in months and it feels fantastic. I actually feel liberated from the burden of the heavy grief shackles that have weighed me down for the past couple of years."

He was right. I knew that, but witnessing someone you love face their own death too soon in life suddenly makes you acutely aware of your own mortality. I wanted to live every minute I had left on earth to the full. However, rather than taking things slowly and relishing every moment, I was living at a frenzied pace, occupying every second I had in an attempt to suppress my grief and sadness.

Given the geographical distance between us – we lived about three hours apart – James and I only saw each other at weekends and holidays. This meant we never endured the day-to-day trials and tribulations of everyday life. This suited me during the first few year or two because it meant I could live my life here and then enjoy the weekends in James's company. Very early into our relationship, James made it clear he had no plans to move 'down south'. In contrast, I had considered moving away from where I lived. Walking around the local area brought back memories which I found increasingly difficult to relive. Everywhere I went, stark reminders of the life I had shared with Ian taunted and goaded me. I wanted to run away, thinking I could start afresh somewhere else.

Meeting James gave me the perfect excuse to run away, even for just the weekend. He also brought the prospect of moving to a new place with a companion who already knew the area.

After about 18 months of seeing each other we were still in the midst of that heart-racing honeymoon stage of our relationship, fuelled by optimism, when I decided to put my house up for sale. I saw this move as being part of my plan to leave the area so I had no regrets about the prospect of moving. When the day came, I knew that driving away from the home I had shared with Ian would be a huge wrench and a small part of me was scared, but the fear was overridden by a desire to start afresh. I loved James and wanted to spend more time with him.

We trawled the online sites and spent many a weekend driving around villages. I saw parts of the country I had never been to before while we searched for a home we could share. As a young child, I had dreamt of owning a property with land where I could keep my horses at home. I imagined looking out at them from my kitchen window while they grazed happily in the pasture beyond. I shared my daydreams with James, who seemed keen to make this a reality for both of us.

After a couple of months I accepted an offer on my house and the hunt for a joint property increased in intensity, but this also put a strain on our relationship. We were moving, quite literally, a little too fast.

We viewed several properties together, but couldn't find one we agreed on. The cracks were beginning to show. James appeared reluctant to move away from the village where he was already resident yet when a property came up to rent only a mile up the road from his house and he suggested we moved in as a temporary option, it was me who baulked at the idea. Perhaps a telling sign that I wasn't as committed to relocating as I thought?

As it happened, the sale of my property fell through. My buyers couldn't get a mortgage and I decided not to pursue the house sale. The house move was put on hold. The stress of potentially moving accompanied by the frequent tiring trips to James's to search for a new home on top of managing a fledgling business while still grieving for my husband took their toll. I finally waved my white flag. Enough was enough. Inside this tough cheery exterior I was crumbling. I needed help before I headed for a nervous breakdown and I needed to try and save my relationship with James.

Chapter 28
You can run but you can't hide

"*D*ear Ian, I feel like crap. My head hurts and I feel sick to the core. I had a hideous phone call with James tonight. Second one in as many days. I think I actually need help. This time of year [January] doesn't help, given its associations with your illness. I'm going to inquire about counselling. I've put on a brave face for far too long and, furthermore, I don't want to hurt James.*"

The real turning point for me, and why I didn't pursue the sale of my house, may seem a little out there, but I knew I had to do something different.

I enlisted the help of an animal communicator who uses a technique called radionics to scan animals for any imbalances or health issues. She does this remotely, using a hair sample and photo. I can hear the doubters among you tutting and rolling your eyes, but stay with me.

My mother-in-law, Pat, had taken her horse, Mulberry, to a horse whisperer and I had been sceptical about the whole thing. Now, however, having experienced 'angel signs', my mind had been opened, albeit through tragic circumstances.

Let me explain further. Having trained as a scientist, I cannot ignore the logical part of my brain. So how do I rationalise my 'kaftan-wafting' tendencies and interest in alternative therapies and communication? Well, let's remember that scientific discoveries are based on data collected from performing experiments based on hypotheses. This 'evidence' either proves or dismisses such hypothetical questions, but do we ever really completely confirm such outcomes? We can only prove something beyond a reasonable doubt based on tests, which, let's face it, are only as accurate as we can make them based on the skills and knowledge we have at that time. Let's also not forget that at one time we thought the earth was flat, until we collected information to suggest otherwise.

Therefore, why can't we believe that other forms of communication exist? Why can't alternative, non-medical forms of treatment work? We may not have the knowledge or skill to provide sufficient evidence to prove this in a recognisable and acceptable form for now. Watch this space, I say.

A fellow horse-riding friend introduced me to Helen after having her own horse assessed. Helen had pinpointed a problem with this horse's spine, indicating the specific affected vertebra, and the vet confirmed the findings. This gave Helen's ability some credence so I contacted her and sent her a few strands of Wilbur's mane for her assessment. He suffered recurrent back pain, which a McTimoney chiropractor treated every few months – the very same lady who had treated Ian. I wanted to see if Helen could add anything further to the picture.

She called me a few days later.

"He's quite special, your boy," she said, having described some areas we needed to address, which concurred with the chiropractor's findings and my experiences from riding him.

"Well, he's very special to me," I responded, and told her how our paths had crossed.

"That makes total sense," Helen continued. "I've never come across a horse before who's more concerned about his owner than his own welfare."

"What do you mean?" I inquired, eager to hear more.

"He's asked me to tell you to stop getting lost in the crowd and start believing in yourself. Get the help you need and keep dreaming. Does that make sense to you?"

"Oh, my beautiful boy," I gulped, overcome with emotion and gratitude. "Yes, I can completely relate to this."

Wilbur's feedback was perfectly timed. I knew what I had to do. As soon as that phone call ended, I rang the hospice and booked bereavement counselling.

"Dear Ian, the last few months have been a living hell. I feel demotivated, lethargic and emotional. It's like having permanent premenstrual tension. I'm still here due to the support of my fantastic friends and because I respect my life so much more after witnessing what you went through. My life and health are gifts and should never be underestimated."

As a self-confessed control freak, counselling doesn't sit well with me. I will happily talk openly about Ian's illness and death, but I very rarely break down or show any emotion while I'm doing so. This is partly for self-protection and partly because I don't want the person I'm speaking with to feel uncomfortable or embarrassed. I know my close friends were sincere when they said I could contact them at any time of day or night if I needed to talk, but asking for help and releasing emotion in front of someone, even a friend, is not something I feel comfortable doing.

Someone once described grief to me as being like a ball trapped within a glass jar.

"Over time," they explained, "the ball will get smaller."

I disagree. I believe the size of the ball doesn't change, the jar gets bigger. In other words, time allows you to rebuild your life around the grief; the pain never goes away, but you learn to manage it better by building a new life around it.

Although I was making good progress in rebuilding my life so far, I was suppressing a lot of pent-up emotion to do so. Now, I had reached a point where I felt I needed professional help to release the quashed feelings within me.

I chose the counselling service offered at the Sue Ryder hospice because I knew they would totally understand my situation and the problems that bereavement brings. I was right. To say those counselling sessions saved me is no understatement. They helped me to recognise my feelings and behaviour were completely normal given the trauma I had experienced. Furthermore, through these fortnightly discussions, I gained clarity about where my heart really lay: my existing home and my friends. I also realised the only reason I continued to event was to try and hang on to the life I'd had cruelly taken away from me. My real passion lay in the sport of dressage.

I gave myself a year to concentrate on settling back into my life at home and shared my intention with James, who, I think, was relieved.

I joined the local hockey club, which not only kept me fit but expanded my social life, too. I moved Wilbur to a new yard run by a fantastic trainer, Grace, who gave me the necessary coaching to improve my skills as a dressage rider. Finally, I was getting my personal life back on track.

Or was I?

My newfound enthusiasm for my life down south meant I became increasingly reluctant to visit James and, over several months, we drifted apart. Perhaps we should have parted ways then, but we limped on in the hope things would get better.

The distance, as well as the fact there seemed to be no plans to move the relationship on, given we were both reluctant to relocate, eventually took its toll. I also realised I had fallen out of love with him. I no longer felt confident by his side. In fact, quite the opposite. I became quieter and more introverted whenever we socialised with friends. The long drive to see him was frustrating and the visits were no longer fulfilling. I didn't look forward to having him stay at mine, either.

"Dear Ian, I have a feeling that James would carry on with us being long distance for the long term, but I'm not prepared to do that. If there's no commitment − or trust − then it's time to walk away. He's better off finding someone local. Ian, give me the strength to do the right thing."

Thanks to the continued counselling, my inner strength was growing. I was discovering who the real Kathryn was − me, without a partner.

Therapy gave me greater clarity about how my people-pleasing tendencies meant I morphed into what I thought the other person wanted, particularly with regards to romantic partnerships. So I lost myself – my true identity. I thought I was being laid-back, easy going. In fact, by not setting personal boundaries, I was teaching the other person that I would just do whatever they wanted, and so my own dreams and ambitions were stagnating.

Over those last few months, James and I were disagreeing more frequently and I wanted to part ways while we were still on reasonably friendly terms rather than after a row or with bad feelings. To me, it felt like being together wasn't making either of us as happy.

After five years, I called time on our relationship.

Apart from the period of time after Ian's death, I had been one half of a couple since the age of 19; pretty much all of my adult life. I wanted to be single for a while – by choice this time. After the initial and inevitable heartache at parting from someone whom I had been so close to for several years, I felt liberated and ready to embrace being single.

I have no regrets about meeting James. He played a valuable part in my recovery. Being with him showed me that I could be in an intimate relationship again. I was beginning to realise that perhaps there was no such thing as 'the one'. Romance has its own timeframe. I'm not the same person I am now as I was when I met Ian, and I have changed considerably over the 10 years since being widowed. I had to grow up, and through the learnings I've gained from rebuilding my life after this tragic loss, I've matured emotionally and become stronger. In fact, I often wonder whether Ian and I would get on in the same way we had, if we met now.

Yes, love was possible in the future, but for the moment, I needed time to work out who Kathryn really was. Grief has its own sense of timing; recovery certainly isn't linear and I wanted space to grieve.

I found the bereavement counselling invaluable on so many levels.

I saw how a long-distance relationship had worked for me at the time. The distance meant I didn't have to fully commit or move the relationship forward, hence the reason we never found a house we both liked. It also meant I could socialise with my friends and live my regular life down south during the week.

There were, and still are, plenty of times that grief still engulfs me, though less frequently these days. The trigger can be a particular song playing on the radio or an emotional scene in a TV show. Sometimes I will feel very angry: angry that Ian died and never realised all his dreams, and that I have been left on my own. I have had nights when I have lain on my bed, punching my pillow in sheer frustration at the unfairness of it all.

"Dear Ian, whenever someone says 'Ian' on the radio or TV or I overhear it mentioned in conversation, it still makes me catch my breath."

Without counselling, I think I would have continued to bottle and suppress all the angst and grief within me – and that isn't healthy.

Part Five

Peeling the Onion of Grief

Chapter 29
Horses and psychotherapy

A few months after finishing my course of bereavement counselling, a regular business client contacted me. We were already in touch about a project I was helping them with, but this was a phone call of a different kind. Lilly had attended a networking event where she met a leadership coach, Pam.

"But that's not all," she continued, clearly eager to tell me more. "Pam uses horses to facilitate her coaching. They are a fundamental part of the coaching process. I immediately thought of you. I know you love horses and from our chats I remembered how much you value coaching."

"Wow!" I breathed. "She sounds very interesting."

"I think you should connect with her," said Lilly determinedly. "I'll send you both an email as an introduction, if that's OK with you?"

"Yes, yes, absolutely," I responded, as my stomach gave a little flutter of excitement.

Firstly, Lilly's kindness blew me away. We already had a great working relationship, but I was touched by her thoughtfulness on a personal level. Secondly, I just knew her chance encounter with Pam was serendipitous.

Following email introductions, during which I described my business and ambitions to Pam, we spoke on the phone. Pam was a not only a coach, but a psychotherapist. Only a few minutes later, her skilled questioning revealed what I really needed.

Tearfully, I described what had happened to Ian and my determination to live in a way that honoured his life.

"I can help you," she said gently. "But it's not business coaching I have in mind to begin with; I think you'd benefit from psychotherapy."

We arranged for me to visit her and the horses at her base in rural Wiltshire.

Three weeks later, I drove through the picturesque Georgian market town of Hungerford before winding my way round the lanes that snaked through this beautiful landscape. I remembered Ian's fascination with this county. I don't know where his love affair for Wiltshire had come from, but I recalled how he said on several occasions he'd like to live there.

I continued my journey through the pretty villages and past the attractive quaint thatched cottages. As I neared my destination, my emotions began to escalate. I felt a lump in my throat and tried to swallow down the tears. My surroundings were already having an impact, drawing me in with their charm and the warming sun streaming through the windscreen. I felt enormous gratitude for being alive.

I turned into the narrow lane that led me to the farmhouse where I would meet Pam. The location was far enough away from civilisation to give the impression you were in the middle of nowhere, but without feeling cut off from the world.

My accommodation for the next two days was an annexe of the main farmhouse, which had its own entrance through French doors and overlooked the garden and paddocks beyond. I unpacked the car and took my sandwiches down to a little bench under a large oak tree in the garden. I sat and closed my eyes, drinking in the blissful heat of the sun. My troubles seemed distant. I felt safe and content.

I met Pam for the first time later that day and found her unassuming, compassionate and kind. We sat down together in a room overlooking the horses' fields and the garden where I had been earlier. Slowly she drew out my story: the absolute bare bones; the raw emotions. Here, I felt able to share every last thread of my tale. I explained how Ian and I had met and what he meant to me. I described the trauma of his illness, the impact of watching him face his own death, of seeing him pass away and how I had since begun rebuilding my life without him.

After getting a good basis from which to work, Pam suggested we went outside to meet the two horses who would participate in my session.

Betty and Clover were quietly grazing in front of us. I took a few deep breaths, inhaling the smell of this glorious countryside, before Pam gently guided me through a meditation. I stood, my eyes closed, and tuned in to the sounds around me – the birdsong, the horses clearing their nostrils and chewing the grass, the hum of the occasional aircraft overhead: sounds we are all usually too busy to notice because of the internal babble going on in our heads.

"And slowly bring your awareness back to your body and open your eyes when you're ready."

I did as instructed, and blinked from the sudden brightness of the sunshine. My whole body felt relaxed, my earlier tears had subsided and I welcomed an inner calmness.

"How are you feeling?" asked Pam, gently.

"Good," I replied. "Really good, thanks."

I did. My troubles had melted away. I felt in that moment as if everything was going to be OK.

"I want you to walk into the paddock and see if you can approach one of the horses. Be very aware of their personal space, and only go as far as you feel is comfortable for you and the horse."

It sounded simple enough, especially given I handled my own horses every day. Yet every time I walked towards either of the mares, they turned and moved off in the opposite direction, creating as much distance as possible between us. After a few minutes, I turned to Pam and shrugged my shoulders.

"They don't seem to want to know me at all," I said, a little sulkily, walking back towards her feeling deflated and defeated.

"This is ridiculous," said a small voice from my mouth as I stood staring at the ground. "I feel unloved."

And there was the real heart of the matter.

My desperation to be accepted and liked was being conveyed through my posture and the mares were picking this up. Horses respond to our non-verbal language because that's how they communicate with each other – and with us, if we're prepared or able to listen. Our body language and tone of voice emit non-verbal cues, of which most of us are completely unaware. Mine was clearly giving off a 'keep away from me' vibe today.

Pam asked me to select one of the mares and walk towards her.

"Try mirroring her posture, so if she has a left leg forward, you put your left leg forward, and be very conscious of her personal space. Stop whenever you feel you are overstepping the mark," she explained.

I did as instructed and became close enough to stroke Clover's nose. Result. I turned back to Pam, standing at the field gate, with a grin on my face, feeling elated.

This single session started a seismic shift inside me. That night, I slept well and awoke feeling refreshed. I felt a huge weight had been lifted from my shoulders. I was even walking taller. After a hearty breakfast, I drove home with the radio turned up loud and sang along to the tunes being played.

I returned to Wiltshire every six weeks for the remainder of the year. The empathy that Pam shared was genuine, truly heartfelt, and my trust in her and the horses continued to grow.

"Dear Ian, I'm at my Wiltshire retreat again. I love it here. I had a fantastic session with Pam and the horses. I was much calmer this time and the feeling of rejection when the horses didn't acknowledge me was much lower. Pam observed how I moved away quickly as soon as the horses walked away from me – she wondered if this was a reflection of how I handled human relationships, too. I'm either intense in my behaviour or disconnected. I think there's a lot of truth in that thought.

We also discussed how I'm always busy, as if keeping my mind occupied helps me to avoid processing the trauma I've experienced. Interestingly, while describing how I felt, I began speaking more quickly and the horses moved further away. With Pam's help, I slowed my breathing and pace of talking down and the horses moved closer to us."

On one occasion, we sat in the middle of the horses' field where the same two mares, Betty and Clover, were grazing. Emotions were high as we discussed Ian's illness once more. I relayed some of the things we'd said to each other during that time, how frightened I had been and how alone I had felt since.

The more angst I released, the closer the horses came/moved to us. By letting go of suppressed feelings, I seemed to be breaking down invisible barriers I'd put around me to protect myself from vulnerability. I was no longer keeping the horses at a distance.

Having made great progress with Pam's help, she suggested I consider some form of energy healing, like biodynamic massage, to complement the talking therapy. While our mental wellbeing benefits from talking things through, our bodies can retain stress following significant and traumatic life changes; energy healing or massage is used to relieve this residual tension found in our body tissue and muscles.

I felt ready to face the next phase of my rehabilitation. My work with Pam had begun the process of self-kindness and self-respect. I owed it to myself to take good care of 'me' so I could continue to get the most out of life and, as it happened, the Universe agreed.

Chapter 30
Quantum energy healing

Following Pam's advice, I explored the internet for a biodynamic massage therapist. My search showed the closest person to me was based several miles away in a busy town. I didn't fancy travelling that distance or to that venue, particularly in the evenings. I knew I wouldn't commit to the regular sessions I needed.

However, my search also picked up a quantum key healing therapist, a treatment offering similar outcomes as biodynamic massage. Furthermore, Louise lived only a couple of miles from me. The way her website was organised, and the way she described what she did, appealed to me and I just knew she was the right person so I booked an appointment.

I immediately warmed to Louise. She had a friendly manner, but seemed a 'no nonsense' type of person. Perfect. We sat down and went through my personal and medical history, which I had sent to her before we met. She asked me how I felt, what I wanted to get out of this session and what challenges I currently faced.

Looking back, I see that my life had already started to shift. Filling in the medical questionnaire, I noted my reluctance to reveal my widowed status. I didn't want to be defined by my loss. This was a first. However, Louise's gentle questioning extracted the real reasons for me being there and, once more, I felt my heart open to release the sadness, fear and shame I'd held within me.

Louise listened to what I said and the words I used, while monitoring posture and facial expressions. If she wasn't convinced by my answer because my non-verbal language was telling her something else, she'd raise her eyebrows and we'd dig a bit deeper until we uncovered the truth.

Bit by bit, she gently and empathetically extracted the problems I faced at that time. My relationship with James had caused me to lose self-confidence, family health issues were concerning me, and there remained a lot of residual grief from Ian's death, far more than I was willing to admit even to myself. Even I had convinced myself that, after eight years, I should have 'got over it'.

Louise applied quantum key energy healing to identify and release areas of tension held within my body. In our first meeting, Louise noted tension in my throat and chest, areas linked with communication. Asthma, something I had been diagnosed with after Ian's death, is a condition that can arise when we don't verbally express our feelings. Louise also found considerable tension in my lower abdomen, also known as the solar plexus, where our bodies accommodate a complex network of nerves and where we store our emotional baggage.

I lay on the treatment couch while Louise placed her hands underneath my back and began the healing process. I felt my back warming up, so much so that Louise's hands were sweating. Then my stomach began to gurgle, signifying the release of anxiety.

I went home feeling great, but within an hour I struggled to swallow. Though alarming at first, I quickly realised this was a reaction to and consequence of the therapy. I knew this symptom would eventually ease, which of course it did.

My reaction to the treatment made sense. I had become skilled at bottling and suppressing my real feelings for so long, not just in relation to Ian's demise, but in other stressful situations throughout my life, to avoid confrontation or having to face the truth.

Thankfully, I have never experienced difficulty in swallowing again, but my response demonstrates the power of energy healing.

With Louise's help, I now understand how I have a propensity to lose myself in a relationship, romantic or otherwise. My people-pleasing tendencies mean I morph into the character I believe will maintain a happy medium. I even did this with Ian. For example, if we ordered a takeaway and I wanted Indian food, but Ian wanted Chinese, I'd acquiesce and go with Chinese. I thought I was being laid back, but all this does, when repeated in different scenarios, is teach the other person that your opinion or choices don't matter. Over time, the other person becomes used to this behaviour and used to getting their way all the time. It's much better to be clear about boundaries in the first place and have a belief in yourself and deal with any confrontation, gently and diplomatically, when and if necessary.

Louise and I have now worked together for two years, over which time I have made significant changes to my life, including having the courage to let go of relationships that were no longer serving me. Recently, I felt able to change my home environment by redecorating, and donating to charity all the brown antique furniture that Ian had collected either through inheritance or his love for auctions. Now my house is filled with light bright traditional oak pieces of my choosing, more accurately reflecting my taste rather than remaining a shrine to my past.

Another major step was removing my wedding ring. For several years after Ian died, I continued to wear Ian's wedding band, which I had had adjusted, along with my engagement ring. Technically, I was no longer married, but in my heart I still was. When I met James, I moved the rings to my right hand out of respect for him, but once that relationship ended, I felt able to remove them completely. I had reached a point where I didn't *want* to wear them anymore. This was the start of a new chapter.

I slid each ring off my finger, one by one, kissed them and placed them gently and carefully in my jewellery box. Ian would remain a significant part of my past, but it was time to move on. Wearing the rings didn't reflect the person I had become.

With Louise's help, I feel more comfortable about moving forwards without guilt about letting go of the past. I am coming to terms with the trauma of losing my husband and I am learning to love who I am. Loving ourselves and putting our needs first – self-care and self-kindness – is something perhaps we all struggle with. Yet, if we don't take care of ourselves, how can we look after or truly love anyone else?

Chapter 31
Reiki healing

Experiencing the power of energy healing sparked a personal interest in other alternative therapies, in particular Reiki – so much so, that I have now trained in Reiki healing and qualified as a Reiki master practitioner, enabling me to use this incredible form of healing to treat humans and horses.

I believe Reiki found me, and has helped me physically and emotionally.

After sustaining a groin strain following a slip during a hockey match, one session of Reiki significantly reduced the pain. This was my first experience of Reiki, and though I had an open mind, even I was shocked at the improvement I felt.

The deeply relaxed state that the Reiki induced was sublime.

Initially, the therapist gently placed her hands in various positions around my head and face. Glorious shades of deep purples, oranges and blues danced within my closed eyelids. A single teardrop rolled down my left cheek as images of dearest Willow, my horse, appeared vividly before me. Thoughts of Ian flooded my mind and more tears trickled down my face. I wanted to swallow frequently, and I wonder if this reflex was similar to what I experienced during Louise's energy healing – another symptom of 'things left unsaid'?

Slowly, the therapist moved her hands over my solar plexus. As she did so, I felt the small of my back start to heat up. I suffer from chronic back pain so I wasn't surprised when this area of my body responded to the healing energy flowing through me.

What I hadn't expected was the extraordinary feeling I had when she reached my feet. My body suddenly felt weightless, like I was floating above the bed. A surge of energy then rippled from my feet up to my head. I felt like my whole body was vibrating before calm descended once more.

When the appointment ended, I surreptitiously asked if the therapist had seen or felt anything. Often, the person giving the healing will also experience sensations.

"Yes!" she exclaimed rather excitedly. "At one point, when I was touching your feet, your whole body became engulfed in a beautiful white light and I felt a wave of energy pass through you."

Not only did I feel more emotionally balanced after this appointment, but my back and groin pain had eased. The discomfort returned a few days later, but was milder. A week or two later, and the groin injury resolved.

I don't fully understand how Reiki healing works, but I believe our bodies respond to the energy, which flows to where it is required. Not only is Reiki lovely to receive, it is wonderful to give.

When I first started practising, I was concerned that I wouldn't be able to feel anything or provide healing. Taster sessions with my friends have increased my confidence and I love being able to help other people feel better.

One friend was going through a tough time both at home and work. She was feeling quite low and I don't think I had appreciated from our conversations just how much she was struggling. I offered her a 10-minute Reiki blast. Just head and shoulders. I worked intuitively, placing my hands to where I felt drawn. When my hands were a small distance away from either side of her temples, an overwhelming rush of sadness swept through me. It was all I could do to stop myself from crying. I continued, moving my hands to above the crown of her head, and felt nauseated, then hot – so hot, in fact, that beads of sweat prickled on my forehead. After 10 minutes I was exhausted, as if my own energy had been drained.

Placing my hands gently on her shoulders to signal the end of the session, I asked quietly, "How are you feeling?"

"Relaxed," she whispered back, but offered nothing else.

If I'm honest, I was a little disappointed that she hadn't described anything more, and again, that nagging doubt gnawed away in my head. Was I just making all this up? However, a few days later, she rang me to tell me she'd booked an appointment to see a psychotherapist, having reached melting point. She thanked me for helping her as she felt the Reiki had released something within her, enabling her to face her worries and fears. Now she is slowly rebuilding her life and self-esteem. I'm so glad that the Reiki healing helped her, at some level, to seek the professional help she so clearly needed.

As I write this, I have completed my equine Reiki level 2 training in which I have learned techniques for applying energy healing to horses. I have already witnessed how my horse, Wilbur, responded to Reiki energy with Kate, my Reiki healer and teacher.

Kate sometimes incorporates drumming into her session so she brought her drum along as well.

It was a beautiful summer's afternoon. The horses were grazing in their field, enjoying the warmth from the sun on their backs. We strolled over to where Wilbur and a couple of his field companions stood under the shade of the trees, lazily flicking their tails against the flies with their heads low and eyes half closed. We sat down on a fallen tree trunk and Kate started a gentle drumbeat.

Wilbur was the first to come and stand closer to us as Kate continued to beat the drum gently, changing the tempo every so often. He lowered his head and pushed his nose towards her so it was just an inch or two away from the stretched animal skin. I swear his muzzle was gently moving to the beat. He closed his eyes and let out a big sigh. I wonder if the vibration of the drum was soothing to him? His companions moved closer too, but stayed a respectful distance around Wilbur. Kate and I smiled at each other as the energy around us softened and we all relaxed in the summer sunshine.

Kate then placed her drum beside her and tuned into Wilbur. Closing her eyes, she held her hands out towards him, feeling the energy flowing between them.

"I can feel something in his throat area," she said as she began to slowly sweep her hands, as if exploring his body from a distance.

"That makes sense," I replied. "Before I bought him, he had an operation on his windpipe to ease his breathing."

"There's also congestion in his gut area," she added, seeming a little more concerned.

"It feels like I need to remove something," she continued, sweeping her hands as if she was extracting an invisible problem from Wilbur's stomach area.

Again, I wasn't surprised by her finding as I had recently wondered if Wilbur was suffering from gastric ulcers. This is a condition that seems to be prevalent in performance horses, particularly if they are worriers, which Wilbur was. A week later I asked my vet to scan Wilbur's gut and stomach ulcers were confirmed.

I truly believe in the power of Reiki healing and hope to continue my path of training and enlightenment in this wonderful energy. Reiki meditation relaxes and quietens my mind, enabling me to tune in to my inner voice, which can only enhance my quality of life.

Chapter 32
Psychic comfort and predictions

P sychic mediums are not everyone's cup of tea, but when a loved one passes, I think our interest is piqued by the possibility of being able to communicate with those we've lost. It took me about five years after Ian's passing before I felt in a place where I was comfortable to try contacting him via this method. A lady was recommended to me by friends.

During that first session, Ian came through and the psychic gave detailed accounts of events and people, relevant to my life, including specifics she couldn't have found out online.

She described Ian accurately in terms of his character and said he was watching over me and always would do.

"He gives you his blessing to move on. In fact, he's pointing to a ring on his finger as if he's indicating marriage in the future. Oh, and now he has kissed your cheek."

My hand instinctively stroked my right cheek and I closed my eyes, imagining his touch.

We discussed future opportunities, including openings for me to write more creatively. She saw me producing three books and writing articles for magazines in the near future. Well, here is the first of the books and I have already created articles for various women's and general interest publications. A house move is likely, with a property being found that's located near water, such as a stream or canal rather than the sea. Quite precise, so we shall see if that comes to fruition. Coincidently, I have always wanted to live in a house by a stream, and another psychic whom I have consulted since repeated the information about buying a home near water and predicted I would author the same number of books.

I found the whole experience comforting and now contact this psychic every six months or so to check in with my own instincts and thoughts rather than as a means of contacting Ian.

Chapter 33
Spirituality and serendipity

Losing Ian made me question everything about my life – my values, my beliefs. Had I done something truly awful in a past life to deserve this? Were we being punished in some way?

I think the appearance of those silver hearts and the other signs I experienced after Ian's death opened my mind – and heart – to spirituality. If these signs were coincidences, then their timing was impeccable. They always turned up whenever I needed comfort and support. I was grateful for the fact I seemed able to connect with him in this way.

I began reading self-help books about spirituality, improving self-esteem, and alternative therapies. Everything I read within them made sense to me, gently guiding me down a path of learning to live in the here and now, to go with the flow, and to trust in a higher force – the Universe, as I prefer to call it – to help me to live the best life I could imagine and desire.

My coaching with Kevin and Elaine increased my awareness of the powers of the Universe. They each enlightened me to the possibility of manifesting the life I wanted just by being very clear about what that looked and felt like. The Universe then works out the 'how'.

The more I became acquainted with this way of living, the more I found things fell into place.

Take, for example, the sale of my horsebox. Ian and I had bought a very basic horsebox when we started eventing. In December 2012, I decided to upgrade and buy a newer model as ours needed an increasing amount of maintenance to keep it on the road. I wanted one with living quarters, so that I could make the most of opportunities to take part in training camps further afield and stay overnight.

I wasn't in any huge hurry so I thought I'd put the Universe to the test and see how events unfolded.

I placed adverts in nearby saddleries and the local veterinary centre, and let my horse-riding contacts know of my plans to sell and what I was looking to buy. I knew, deep down, that everything would fall in place. I truly felt that.

Sure enough, after a month or so of inquiries about my lorry that didn't lead to any sale, I received an email from my horsebox mechanic, Simon, who knew of a truck that met my requirements. Even better, he had built said vehicle for the current owner and he kindly offered to give it a once over before I purchased it. I went along to view it and instantly knew it was the one for me. Simon's inspection supported this decision and within a couple of weeks, I had negotiated a good discount on the price and became the proud owner.

But what about my old lorry?

Well, Simon had already given me a Plan B, with a cash offer for scrap if I didn't sell it. However, the Universe was looking after me once more, as a buyer rang me a week after the new horsebox arrived. He happened to live up the road from me, we had many mutual contacts within the local equestrian community and not only did he buy my lorry, he has since helped me with some home and car maintenance.

The more I learn to live like this, the more people I meet who are also aware of these laws of attraction.

Not so long ago, I decided to treat myself to a make-up lesson. Now in my 40's – and possibly going through a mid-life rebellion – I decided it was time to learn how to make the best of my appearance. On the recommendation of a friend, I travelled to Milton Keynes for an hour-long tutorial in a large department store. Not being a great fan of clothes shopping, this was the first time I had been back to the mall where Ian bought his spectacles.

I felt emotions stirring within me as I entered the centre, where weekday shoppers and workers were making the most of their lunch hour freedom. I smiled as I saw the familiar green signage of Marks and Spencer and felt, strongly, that Ian was cheering me on as I ventured way out of my comfort zone and into the brightly lit department store.

Expecting to be ushered into a room away from the shop floor, I was somewhat alarmed when the young lady who greeted me at the counter escorted me to a chair in front of a large mirror – right in the middle of the stand and in full view of the public. Oh, this was so not what I had had in mind! I tried self-reassurance:

"No-one is interested in what I'm doing. Everyone is too busy shopping to even notice me."

No. My inner dialogue was having little impact. My body gave my real feelings away as sweat rendered my palms clammy while moisture left my throat in a panic.

"Nice one, Ian," I muttered before smiling politely through the mirror at my make-up instructor, Charlene, who beamed back at me as she approached.

My anxiety was soon soothed by the instant rapport I felt with Charlene. A beautiful woman who, I knew, being only a few years younger than me, would totally understand my make-up needs. She began with the basics, and as the session progressed, and my confidence grew, I found myself revealing more about my background, including the loss of my husband. She listened intently and though she hadn't shared the same tragedy, she had had her own succession of hurdles to overcome.

Pleased with my new look, I asked Charlene to gather the products she had used so that I could purchase them. Off she went, and I stood up to put my coat on when a woman appeared at my shoulder.

"I wanted to come over to tell you that your eyes look amazing," she told me. "I've been stood the other side of the stand watching the transformation, and you look incredible."

Well, if ever I needed an endorsement for having had the nerve to complete this tutorial, there it was.

"Thank you very much," I replied. "I was really nervous about doing this, especially in full view of everyone, so your comments mean a lot."

I relayed what had happened to Charlene when I arrived at the cash desk.

She gave me a knowing look, before saying, "That'll be the laws of attraction at work then."

I laughed back. "Oh, without a doubt."

Not only did she give me her number in case I ever needed a make-up artist, she gave me an additional discount on my purchases and pre-ordered a copy of this book.

Through my exploration of spirituality, I've become an avid user of a psychic pendulum. I find it an invaluable tool for making decisions. It was Janie, the editor of the online eventing magazine, who introduced me to this during a visit to her home shortly after Willow's demise. She had discovered this technique – along with the laws of the Universe – after the death of her father and a close friend.

She placed a box containing small bottles of various flower remedies on her kitchen table and produced a crystal, the size of a cherry tomato, attached to one end of a thin thread. She held onto the other end of the thread with the thumb and forefinger of one hand and suspended the crystal over the box of bottles.

"Am I sat in my kitchen with Kathryn?" she asked out loud.

Her hand stayed perfectly still, but the pendulum began to swing left and right. Given we knew the answer to this question was yes, the pendulum was now calibrated: it would swing left and right for 'yes', and swing up and down, away from Janie, for 'no'.

Slowly, she moved the crystal over each bottle and for three out of the twenty, the swing indicated 'yes'. She extracted the chosen remedies and, reading the small print, I wasn't surprised to see that they were essences known to aid grief and sadness.

Intrigued, I asked, "So, who or what is causing this to crystal to swing? Does it connect to spirits – to people we've lost?"

At that time, I was rather hoping it was a way of contacting Ian.

"I like to think so," she replied, as she dangled the crystal over the box once more. "Let's see if there are any other essences you need."

One more bottle was chosen by virtue of the crystal swinging left and right. Janie picked it out of the box and her eyes widened as she read the label. She turned it around for me to see.

"I think you have your answer about who we've connected to today," she smiled.

The label read: 'Willow'.

That was it. I needed no more convincing and I continue to use a psychic pendulum on a weekly basis as a way of connecting with my subconscious mind. Sometimes you just need to breathe, and trust your gut feelings, and this little pendulum enables me to do just that.

My spiritual journey continues and I love the feeling of freedom I get from going with the flow and being more in tune with, and trusting of, the Universe to guide me. There are still times when my 'internal planner' tries to control events or outcomes or I feel impatient and frustrated when things don't go the way I had expected or outcomes take too long to come to fruition. The difference now is that I acknowledge these feelings and let them be rather than berating myself for being imperfect!

I wouldn't call myself religious – being a member of an organised religion doesn't appeal to me, though I understand why some people may seek this path. Being spiritual and believing in the power of the Universe are terms I feel more comfortable with. I think my love of horses partly stems from the spiritual connection these beautiful animals seem to have – a deep wisdom and sixth sense – which fascinates me, particularly having coached alongside them with Pam's help.

Working with therapists, Louise and Pam, continues my spiritual enlightenment and Reiki meditation is another perfect method by which I can quiet my mind, alongside regular yoga practice. These continue to be a fundamental part of my recovery, helping me to feel more at peace with myself and the world around me.

I've also grown in terms of my inner strength, and matured emotionally. I can see how I expected James to fill the void that opened up within me after Ian's death. I freely admit that at the time we met, I wanted to be rescued, for someone to heal my pain, which is never a robust starting point to any relationship, romantic or otherwise. I suspect the initial intensity of that relationship was suggestive of a mutual need for love and attention: an attraction borne from a shared cry for support.

Through the work I've done on myself by means of voracious reading of my self-help library and the counselling and therapy, I know that I will start any future relationship from a much healthier and more content place. Embarking on a romantic journey always involves an element of risk, but it is unhealthy – and unreasonable – to be totally dependent on another person. I firmly believe that if I'm true to myself, and love my life as it is, then any relationship will be a gift rather than a necessity, resulting in deeper and lasting connection.

It's wonderful – and freeing – to feel so in tune with my intuition, to be happy with who I am and to enjoy my life as it is.

Part Six

Animal Healers and Heartbreakers

Chapter 34
Puppy love

N
ow that I was working from home and my business was established, my dream of owning a dog could finally become a reality. After all, I had my horses and my cat – just the dog and canary to find now in order to complete my childhood dream. And, right on schedule, in March 2015, a very special litter of puppies came into the world.

Grace, my dressage trainer, had bred from her lovely little terriers, Beryl and Terence, resulting in seven adorable puppies.

A week after they were born, I was riding Wilbur when Grace appeared at the door of the school, carrying a little black bundle. It was one of the puppies. Having dismounted, I led Wilbur over to see her.

"Here you go," she said, beaming, as she handed the sleepy little fur ball to me.

"Oh no!" I exclaimed. "Don't do this to me – I won't be able to resist."

Sure enough, the puppy, with a white flash on his chest, wriggled into the crook of my arm, made a little noise of contentment and fell back asleep.

"Oh, little fella," I breathed in. "He looks like a mole."

There and then, my heart melted. I held him for a few more minutes before reluctantly handing him back to Grace, whereupon he licked my finger. That was the deal sealed; he was mine.

I had to do the sensible thing and meet all the puppies just to make sure, but I knew 'Mole' was the one for me. How had Grace known?

She generously let me visit him on a regular basis over the next eight weeks until he was ready to come home with me. Each time I went to see him, he would readily leave his brothers and sisters to come over and greet me. When I picked him up for a cuddle, he would wriggle his way up to my neck, snuggle in and snooze. I had fallen well and truly under the spell of this little chap.

I won't lie – the first month after he came home was testing and tiring. Toilet training was the first challenge and I was thankful that the weather was getting warmer and drier as we moved further into spring and then summer. Every half an hour, I'd carry Mole outside into the back garden and say the magic words, 'wee wee', as instructed by the puppy training book I had read before his arrival.

Slowly, over a few weeks, we were able to expand the amount of time between garden visits and he began to stand by the back door when he needed to go out. Clever boy!

Seeing his confidence increase and his training improve was very rewarding. He was thoroughly entertaining to watch while he played – running around the house with a soft toy in his mouth which invariably squeaked or rattled, depending on what was inside it. I kept my work schedule light, which meant that I could play with him while he was full of beans and then catch up on work when his energy levels suddenly crashed and he'd curl up in his bed asleep. Given I'm more of a lark than a night owl, I bought several DVDs to keep me awake until 11 pm so Mole could manage his way through the night without needing a loo break.

Fortunately, Harry the cat accepted him too. Mole was so small when he came home that Harry asserted his authority early on. Having said that, the pair made me laugh during the summer months, when they'd chase each other around the lawn: one minute Harry would chase Mole and the next they'd swap around. I wouldn't say they're best friends, but they have a healthy respect for each other and rub along together fine. At night, they often curl up with me on the bed.

Yes, I know, it didn't take long.

To begin with, Mole slept in a crate in the kitchen. That arrangement lasted five months until he decided to howl at 2 am each morning. I don't know what the cause of this was, but that and the fact it was getting harder for me to say goodnight and leave him meant I relented and took him upstairs to bed, where he's slept ever since.

Never have I regretted my decision to bring this small bundle of joy home.

What I hadn't expected was the profound effect this little hound would have on my self-confidence, and how many lovely people I would meet as a consequence of having him in my life. I feel like I can achieve anything.

Even the loneliness I had experienced following Ian's death was becoming much less frequent. Living on my own, I had found the summer evenings particularly lonesome if I sat out in the garden. I think it's because I could hear my neighbours chatting with family and friends or laughter from the pub garden, which made me feel even more alone. In winter, being inside seems more acceptable, cosied up in front of the fire with the curtains drawn, like everyone else. Yet I love being outdoors so having Mole gave me confidence to sit outside and make the most of the lighter, warmer evenings.

Having Mole soothed the feelings of solitude in other ways, too. We attended weekly puppy training classes for the first year – not only great for socialising the dogs, but humans as well. Our trainer has become a good friend and we often bump into the other puppies, and their owners, on our walks around the local area.

Having a dog has not only given me a perfect excuse to explore the beautiful countryside around us, but other people, dog-walkers or not, always stop to talk. He's a particular hit with the staff at the dog-friendly coffee shops I frequent with my laptop to write.

I've even started running because I now have a training buddy and we've joined the local canicross club. Canicross is a sport in which you run attached to your dog by a harness and lead, so they effectively pull you along. What an incredible adrenalin-fuelled experience that is. Mole doesn't run like this very often due to his small stature, but the lovely friends I've made offer me their larger dogs to run so I still feel a part of the group. In the summer months, we all go swimming with our dogs at a local water park and enjoy paddle boarding with the dogs beside us on the boards.

I love going on holiday with Mole, too. Our favourite spot is the North Norfolk coast. Watching him race around on the sand and paddle in the sea makes my heart swell.

He is my best friend and I cannot imagine life without him or another dog in the future. He brings out my fun side and I love him to pieces. Mole is a great life coach, too, because if ever you needed to see evidence of living in the moment, watch a dog. Their attention is always on whatever is going on at that point in time, whether it's chasing a ball, eating food or sniffing the hedgerows.

"When God created you, he was in a very good mood," I often say to him as he fixes me with his kind brown eyes and cocks his head on one side as if he understands every word I'm saying to him.

How I wish Ian could have met him. He grew up around dogs – his parents always had black Labradors – so I know he would have fallen in love with this madcap terrier of mine. But then, I like to think he has met Mole because I believe animals are far more sensitive to spirit than us humans. I often catch Mole – and Harry – staring into the corner of a room, as if seeing something – or someone – and I wonder if they detect a spiritual presence that I can't see. I hope so and I do believe that in some parallel Universe, Mole and Ian have already met

Chapter 35
Goodbye Moose

While animals give an untold amount of joy, they also cause their own share of heartache, as I had already experienced with the passing of Willow.

Moose had taken well to retirement, spending his time out in the field with his friends. However, six years on and the cold weather of winter began to take its toll on him. He was losing weight despite eating large quantities of food and wearing thick rugs to keep him warm. Aged around 18 years, he wasn't particularly old for a horse, but my intuition was telling me he was preparing to move on. In fact, I'd stand with him in the field and talk to him, letting him know that I was fine, that if he felt it was time to leave and be back with Ian, then I would cope.

As it happened, in December of that same winter, he cut his leg on the fencing that enclosed his field. The head girl at the stables called me.

"We've brought Moose in from the field. I don't think it's too serious, but I would get it looked at by the vet just to be on the safe side."

The vet came and confirmed that, although the wound didn't require stitching, antibiotics were needed to safeguard against infection. We bandaged his leg and stabled him for the next week until we were sure any risk of further complications had passed.

The very fact that Moose was happy to be confined within a stable was another alert that all was not well. Having taken so well to being out in a field all day and night, I realised just how much he suffered from claustrophobia. He had been trying to tell Ian and me since we got him that he wasn't happy being confined within a stable, but we had misinterpreted his behaviour as being cheeky. He would occasionally 'box walk' – walk round and round his stable - or he'd head-butt us if we stood too close, but he always loaded onto the horsebox, where he was even more confined, so we didn't think anything more of it.

Since being outdoors 24/7, his anxiety in the stable had become more notable and that's why I linked the two together. Now, with whatever was going on inside his body, he was more than happy to be in the warm and dry, and even became reluctant to walk outside. Something wasn't right with dear old Moosie.

I visited him at least twice a day to change his dressings, administer antibiotics, clean his bedding and feed him. Despite this intensive care and regular vet visits, his wound wasn't healing. If anything, it was getting worse. Infection wasn't evident, but it was as if his skin wasn't capable of healing. His weight was still dropping, drastically.

"Dear Ian, what is going on with Moose? I'm worried about him. His health seems to be deteriorating. Please let me do the right thing for him. He's a very, very special boy. I think he misses you, my darling."

There are limits to the amount of food that horses can digest in any 24-hour period and Moose was on maximum rations. Even with his increased calorie intake and lack of exercise, his ribs were becoming more visible. Blood samples didn't reveal anything alarming. A rectal examination indicated a growth on one side of his gut, but gave no other clues as to what was going on. Additional, more invasive tests were required to get an accurate diagnosis. Given his poor condition and the fact he was now struggling to walk, I didn't want to stress him even more by transporting him to the veterinary centre. For me, it didn't seem ethical to put a very poorly horse through more trauma and in an unfamiliar environment.

"Dear Ian, I feel a shift in relation to Moose. I believe he's preparing to move on – to be with you. He has looked after me for the past six years and I think he now knows I'm stronger and no longer holding onto him because of what he represents."

The vet agreed with me. There was nothing more that we could do to make him better and so I made the heart-wrenching decision to put my beautiful boy, my last link with Ian, to sleep.

On his last day, I went up to the yard in the morning to say my goodbyes and found a bowl full of carrots, parsnips and apples placed outside his stable. The lovely ladies on the yard had gathered all these goodies together for Moose's last meal. This small gesture of kindness made me cry even more. Moose had clearly touched them all and they'd fallen for his laid-back Irish charm.

I sat with my boy as he tucked in to this equine culinary delight, unaware of his fate. I stroked his long chestnut neck and buried my face in his mane to inhale his smell. I knew that letting him go was the kindest act I could do under the circumstances, but it didn't make the decision to put him down any easier.

I felt he was saying back to me, "Kathryn, you are stronger now. I have looked after you for the past few years to make sure you were ok. It is time for me to be with Ian again. Please, let me go."

I relished those final moments with him, remembering with such fondness the pleasure this big chestnut horse had given Ian and me.

As he munched his hay, I kissed his neck one more time and whispered, "Goodbye Moosie. Now, gallop free, sweet boy, and be with your true master once more."

Reluctantly, I left his stable. I had been advised by friends not to be around when the vet came so that I could remember Moose as he was. Plus, I didn't want him to pick up on my anguish. I knew he'd pass away far more peacefully if I wasn't there.

"Dear Ian, I'm so glad that you and Moose are reunited. I couldn't let him deteriorate further. I imagine the pair of you galloping over the fields with big smiles on your faces."

Chapter 36
Wilbur the champion

With Moose no longer with me, I focused on Wilbur's training. Under Grace's guidance, we were growing in confidence and making great progress with our dressage.

I had entered Wilbur for a dressage competition, the day after travelling back from friends. Not the best planning on my part as I was tired, and the cold, damp and grey morning did nothing to stoke my enthusiasm. The wind was icy and my fingers became increasingly numb as I struggled to plait Wilbur's mane. I cursed under my breath as another plaited piece of mane sprang free from my grasp. Why the hell was I going out on a day like this? Not a spark of excitement was evident as I packed the horsebox and prepared Wilbur to travel. I should have stayed at home, but I'd paid the entry fee and I wasn't going to wimp out now.

My friend Jules came with me to help so I had good company.

Thirty minutes before I was due in the arena, I mounted and rode over to the collecting ring to warm Wilbur up. He seemed a little tense to begin with, but I didn't think this unusual given the arctic temperatures combined with the fact we were among several other horses. I persevered, and he began to relax.

"Kathryn White, you are next," announced the steward.

I acknowledged her request and walked Wilbur down to the next arena where we would ride our test.

"Good luck!" called Jules as she went to stand by the side to watch.

The judge rang her bell and we began our test. All seemed to be going well until I asked for canter. Once more, Wilbur seemed tense and unwilling to go forwards. I urged him on with my leg and that was it, he exploded. He bucked so high that I swear he did a handstand. The force unseated me and I soared into the air, landing heavily on my backside in the sand and narrowly missing a head injury as Wilbur lashed out with a hind leg before cantering off up the arena.

"Arrrrrrghhhhhhh!" I gave out a low groan and lay back on the cold sand.

I felt winded, and my back was throbbing intensely. After a few minutes, I slowly and gingerly rolled over onto all fours. The intensity of pain that fired up my back was beyond anything I'd ever experienced and I was struggling to get my breath.

Having stood with her mouth open in utter shock at Wilbur's antics, Jules came running over to me.

"What can I do to help?" she asked.

"Give me a second," I replied, my eyes closed.

Despite the agony I was in, I couldn't help feeling bad that I was holding up the rest of the competition. I needed to summon the strength to move from the arena and clear the area.

The steward came over and suggested they call a paramedic.

"No," I muttered, eyes closed, focusing on not passing out. "No, I'll be absolutely fine. I've just winded myself, but it's easing now."

"Would you like me to rub your back?" asked Jules, desperately wanting to ease my discomfort.

"Oh, yes, please. Gas and air? Gin and tonic?" I managed a wry smile.

"Always the comedian," smiled Jules as she sympathetically rubbed my back to try and ease the obvious pain I was in.

With help, I managed to stand, my legs still wobbly and weak.

Not only did I stupidly refuse paramedic help, but also the kind offer of stabling for Wilbur. I just wanted to get him back to the yard, go to bed and rest, in the belief that I'd tweaked a back muscle and all would be OK in the morning. I gratefully accepted a hot black sweet cup of coffee, loaded Wilbur back onto the lorry and drove – yes, drove – home. Not only that, but with Jules's help, I unloaded all the tack and equipment from the horsebox, mucked out and hung heavy hay nets up in Wilbur's stable before settling him down for the night.

Back home, I couldn't get comfortable. Painkillers were not living up to their name. I tried lying on my back with my legs over a chair, which gave me some relief for a few minutes, and then I had to find another position in which to sit or lie. Lying in a hot bath seemed to be the only solution and I must have had about four or five baths over the course of that evening. Eventually, I crawled on my hands and knees up the stairs to bed, hoping that sleep would provide me with a few hours of respite.

The next morning I awoke early – around 6 am – with a dire need for more pain relief. I slowly eased my legs out of the duvet and over the side of the bed before gingerly sitting up. I gasped as pain shot up my back. Oh, this was pure agony. The only way I could move was on all fours. I suddenly felt very alone and frightened; all the bravado I had mustered yesterday to get Wilbur and myself home dissipated as I crawled to the phone to call Jules and ask her to take me to A&E.

There, X-rays showed I'd suffered a compression fracture of my T12 vertebra and I was under strict instructions from my consultant to lie in bed on my back and not move.

"I've got animals who need looking after," I moaned. "Can't you send me home in a brace or something and some medication for the pain?"

"Young lady, you are very lucky to be walking. If your fracture hadn't been stable, you would be in a wheelchair," was the stern response.

I burst into tears. I'd really done myself a mischief this time. How I wished Ian was with me. He'd have known what to do. He'd have put everything right.

I lay on my back for four days in the hospital ward, counting ceiling tiles, worrying about the business, about my animals, about how I was going to manage when I returned home. Meanwhile, the medical staff performed further scans, which indicated that, thankfully, I didn't need any metal pins or further intervention.

My fantastic friends came to visit me daily and made sure my little furry menagerie was cared for in my absence. Despite the consultant's stern words, my stubborn streak kicked in the second day I was on the ward. A few friends had visited me that day and they sat around all three sides of my bed, chatting away to me, updating me with all the gossip and news. After a while, I began to feel nauseous from having to move my head to see who was talking. One friend noticed the colour drain from my face as I struggled to focus on the conversation around me.

"Right, come on, I think it's time we left and let Kathryn rest," she announced, ushering them away from my bedside, before dropping back and asking me if I was OK.

"Yes," I replied weakly. "I'll be fine. I just need to sleep."

That evening, I drifted in and out of consciousness or sleep, I don't know which. I just knew that I wanted to be discharged as soon as possible. I remembered back to when Ian had been desperate to come home and how the nurses had told him to drink lots of water to stay hydrated. I asked the nurses for some orange juice and water, which I sipped through a straw given my horizontal position. When they came round, periodically, to check my blood pressure, I lied and said I was OK when they thought it was a little low. I know it was stupid and I risked having to stay even longer, but at that moment, all rational thought left me and I just wanted to go home at whatever cost.

I remained in hospital for five days and credit to my fantastic clients, who all incorporated a week-long delay into their schedules to keep me on their projects. I'll never forget when, on the day of discharge, I had to demonstrate that I could walk the 20 metres or so from my bed to the window of the ward. I was shocked at how light-headed and sick I felt from sitting up for the first time after only a few days lying down.

It was certainly a drastic wake-up call for me to slow down and this time, I took heed. I had no choice really.

For the next three months, I wore a brace that looked like a police stab vest, morning and night, so that I didn't bend or twist my back and make it worse. I wasn't allowed to drive for two of those months, either. Once more, my friends rallied around, driving me to the shops or washing my hair, or just sitting with me and having a natter. Thankfully, I was able to work though I could only sit at my desk for short periods before backache kicked in.

After those first three months, I slowly increased the amount of time without the back brace and, with the help of physiotherapy, began rebuilding my core strength.

Five months later, and the consultant signed me off and agreed that I could start riding again. I went up to the stables a week later, feeling very apprehensive about getting back in the saddle. The first time I rode again, I mounted and sat there for a minute or two, surprised by how emotional I felt. Grace walked beside me, holding onto a lead rope attached to Wilbur's bridle. We repeated this over the next week until I felt confident enough to let Grace remove the lead rope and increase her distance away from me. With her continued help and encouragement over the next month, I was able to walk, trot and canter independently again and my confidence levels continued to improve over the following six months.

The time off work seemed to have done Wilbur good, and he was performing better than he had ever done. Given he was now showing no apparent signs of discomfort after his rest, I put the incident down to being 'just one of those things' and cracked on.

My determination to ride again and continue Wilbur's training was rewarded when, 18 months after my accident, he became Medium Level Dressage Champion at a regional competition and was placed sixth at a national competition.

Sadly, our glory was short lived.

About four months after those achievements, he became increasingly unpredictable and dangerous to ride. I knew he wasn't being naughty. He loved his work so something was clearly wrong. He had regular chiropractic appointments, but nothing seemed to be helping.

After a particularly dangerous incident in which he unexpectedly reared bolt upright – I fell off and was lucky to escape with only a dislocated thumb – I had him referred to the Animal Health Trust, a specialist veterinary practice, because I knew, deep down, something more sinister was the cause.

The veterinary team there performed a whole host of tests and concluded that he was in considerable pain when ridden due to issues in his legs and back. He could be rested and brought back in to gentle work, but given his unpredictable and dangerous reaction, I was advised to retire him completely. So that's what I did.

The time off work he'd had while I recovered from the back injury probably eased his pain and gave us a little while longer before his discomfort worsened, hence his unpredictable behaviour. He retired a champion and owed me nothing. Wilbur and I had been on an incredible journey together, during which we reached a level of training I had never achieved before.

He spent the summer months out in the field with his friends, which he absolutely loved. Unfortunately, he did rather too well out on grass and severe laminitis crippled him.

Laminitis is a painful condition that involves inflammation of the feet. It is a complex disease with several possible causes and is being researched extensively by the equine veterinary community. Too much rich grass has been linked with the illness, though other possible causes are now likely. Part of the treatment process is restricting the amount of grass eaten by the afflicted horse.

Given the severity of Wilbur's laminitis, it was looking increasingly likely that he would have to spend the rest of his life stabled, with limited access to grazing. Once more, I felt fate was guiding me. This was not how I wanted my horse to exist. I consulted my vet and farrier and decided the kindest act for my dear Wilbur was to put him to sleep. And, just to make my decision that little bit easier, he sustained a nasty injury from being kicked by another horse in the field, making him even more lame and uncomfortable.

On his last morning, I turned him out into the paddock by his stable so he could enjoy grazing with the sun on his back. I wanted this to be his final memory. I carried Mole in my arms into the field so we could say farewell to our friend together.

Wilbur and Mole got on very well. Wilbur would lower his head to say hello to Mole who would then lick Wilbur's nose. This morning, my horse's coat was glistening, dark and beautiful. What a stunning horse. I held out an apple and he blew softly on my hand through his nostrils before gently taking the fruit. I stood stroking his sleek neck, unable to contain myself anymore. I wept as I stood there with my boys, Mole lying quietly in my arms.

I don't know how long we stood there before I became aware that the yard had gone very quiet. The girls had stopped taking the other horses past us to the fields. I realised my friends were kindly giving me the time and space to say my goodbyes to this special boy. Reluctantly, I turned my back and walk out of that field. Not only was this a heart-breaking farewell to my beautiful best friend, but this was yet another goodbye to my past life.

Chapter 37
I find Barry White

It wasn't long before a new equine friend found me. Baz, aka Hestedora, joined my little clan shortly after Wilbur's passing. Given Wilbur's retirement, I had already decided to look for another horse to ride and compete.

Now in my forties and with some savings set by, I felt it was now or never to look for a talented horse specifically bred for dressage to build on what I'd already learned.

Grace recommended her trainer of 20 years as a potential source for such a horse and we arranged to go over to Holland to see him for the day. I received a couple of videos beforehand of two youngsters he had for sale who might be suitable. One was a five-year old mare, the other a gelding who was only four. Based on the video footage, I was convinced I would buy the mare and dismissed the gelding on the basis he was too young for me.

On the day of our trip, the alarm clock's shrill tones awoke me at 4 am. The sky was pitch black, but I was too excited to worry about the early start. Harry uncurled himself from his sleeping position at the foot of my bed and purred happily as he rubbed up against my pyjama-clad leg. Mole was already with his dog sitter.

"It's your lucky day," I said to Harry, bending to stroke his silky soft fur. "An early start for you to catch some extra mice."

It was too early for breakfast so, after washing and dressing, I got in the car to go and pick up Grace en route to the airport. The radio fired up and guess what song was playing? 'Tulips of Amsterdam'. Surely that was a good sign?

Our flight was trouble free and following a short train ride through the Dutch countryside, Grace and I arrived in the small town of Houten. We sat waiting for our lift to the stables and our conversation turned to Rio; the Olympics were due to start later that same week. I related a story about Ian going there on a business trip, during which he visited Copacabana beach. Then, bizarrely (I blame too much coffee) we both burst into song, singing Barry Manilow's hit of the same name. Thankfully, our lift arrived before we gave an encore.

Ten minutes later, we arrived at the stables and met the two horses – the first being the four-year old gelding I had dismissed.

"What's he called?" asked Grace, as this beautiful bay came over to say hello.

"Berry," was the response, but with the speaker's lovely accent it sounded like 'Barry'.

"Oh, how spooky is that?" I asked Grace; clearly Barry was still on our minds from our impromptu duet.

The name Barry stuck, and he clearly liked fuss and attention. I loved him. He seemed to have a very sweet nature.

In contrast, the mare was more interested in her hay than us. She didn't turn round to say hello and carried on munching, her attention elsewhere. I can't even remember her name because my mind was very much still on 'Barry'.

The feelings continued when I rode them both. The mare was beautifully trained and stunning to look at, but I didn't feel any connection with her. Barry, on the other hand, had joy written through him like a stick of seaside rock. Despite his tender years, he gave me a wonderful feeling. I felt he was saying, "What next? Come on, let's have some fun."

Grace liked him, too. I'd found my future horse, I felt sure of it. Several times that day, I went into his stable for a cuddle.

However, when I returned home, self-doubt crept in and I began to question my ability to take on such a young and talented horse. Why was I wavering? He had been trained beautifully so far, but was I confident enough to train him further?

He passed the pre-purchase veterinary examination, so it was now crunch time and the only person who could make the decision to buy him was me. My gut instinct was telling me to go ahead. I knew I would enjoy spending time with this horse... What was I to do? I quietened my mind using my Reiki meditation.

It took a few minutes before a light bulb flashed in my mind. Of course. I recalled how Ian and I had found Moose. We had been so naïve about buying horses back then and bought a horse with no record of where he came from or any information about his breeding. He was also much younger than we'd anticipated buying, not to mention a lot bigger than either of us would have liked, and he hadn't had as much training as Barry at that point. Yet, Ian had believed in Moose and look at the pleasure that horse had brought us since.

Decision made. Barry White – Baz - was coming home.

He arrived a week later and my instincts were spot on. He is an absolute joy to own and ride. I love going to see him every day; he's a complete time waster given he enjoys attention and cuddles. Everyone on the yard has fallen for his sweet, gentle nature. For a four-year old he's very chilled out, although occasionally he'll push the boundaries just to remind me he's so young. I cannot wait to see where our journey takes us. He has no link to my past, only my future, and that feels right. No matter what happens, Baz has a home for life with me.

Chapter 38
Giving something back and creating a legacy

S o, my path is, for now, journeying along the dressage route, but I still get my eventing fix by organising an annual competition in Ian's memory. I wanted to create a legacy in Ian's name to support amateur event riders like ourselves and give something back to the sport we had both been so passionate about. The first Ian White Memorial Trophy was awarded in 2009 and the event is now held annually in the picturesque setting of Windsor Great Park as part of the Smiths Lawn Horse Trials. I chose this venue because it is in Ian's home county of Berkshire and was one of our favourite competition venues. Furthermore, the organiser was a staunch supporter and regular reader of our Team White column.

The winning rider of our class must be an amateur rider, which means they have no commercial sponsors to fund their competing, and they must own the horse they are riding. Our class has gained popularity over the years and we now have a waitlist.

The first event was particularly poignant as, yet again, Ian made his presence known to me with several lovely signs.

"Dear Ian, the big day is almost here and I'm feeling increasingly emotional. More wobbly than normal. I don't regret organising this event; it totally depicts you and your love for eventing and I completely believe in this venture, but I know it's going to unleash a whole new load of bloody grief demons because you're not here beside me."

In addition to the main trophy, we awarded a silver salver to the best turned-out horse and rider – the ones who looked the most neat and tidy. One combination stood out for me, not only because of the rider's impeccable turnout, but also because she was riding a bay mare who looked very much like my own Willow. In addition, she had carefully stencilled a Tudor rose onto her mare's hindquarters. These 'quarter marks' are created by brushing the horse's coat in different directions. The rose caught my Lancastrian eye and I smiled. I knew this was a sign from Ian, but would this horse and rider do well in the competition?

They completed the show jumping phase with a clear round so added no penalties to their overall score.

Now it was on to the final phase, the cross-country round. I made my way to the warm-up arena in time to see them set off. The rider was wearing green – also my cross-country colours – and her commentary biography could have been written by me to describe Willow. She had posted a great score after the dressage and given her clear round in the show jumping; she was lying in first place. She held her nerve and crossed the finish line without picking up any more penalties to win.

Her victory was even more touching when we discovered her motivation to enter the competition. She emailed me to thank me for her trophy and prizes, and then came the bombshell.

"My young nephew died of a brain tumour a few months before this event and his death gave me the added encouragement to enter. I felt his presence beside me all that day, he spurred me on."

Chapter 39
A sting in the tale

I n a strange and tragic twist of fate, a dear friend of mine is now facing the same hideous hell I did. Her husband was diagnosed with a grade 4 GBM brain tumour in January. Eleven months later, Chloe's husband passed away, at home and with his beautiful wife by his side, just a year after his initial symptom, a bad limp in his right leg, became apparent.

Who would have predicted this when we met in 2009?

Listening to her daily struggles over the past year, I wondered how I had managed to get through the months of Ian's illness. All those fears and emotions came flooding back to me, but given it's almost 10 years now since Ian's death, I can also see how far I've come.

Being there for Chloe through this year has been an opportunity for me to give back and offer my love to a dear friend. I feel I've been able to indirectly say thank you to all those lovely people who supported me.

I will continue to be by Chloe's side as she rebuilds her life. She, too, is spiritual, and we enjoy sharing thoughts about life, the Universe and yoga. We also have a lot of laughs, too; laughing in the face of life's absurdities.

This year, spurred on by her plight, I completed my first half marathon to raise money for the charity Brain Tumour Research. If you'd told me a few years ago that I'd be running any distance, let alone 13 miles, I would have thought you'd lost your marbles. Wearing my bright pink charity t-shirt, with my name emblazoned front and back, there was no way I wasn't going to finish that race.

The long hours of training required even for a half-marathon wouldn't have been as much fun without the support, encouragement and banter from Gazza Gazelle, Whizzy Watts, Plaity and Francis (no nickname – yet). The first two made sure I conquered my fear of hills – nothing to do with heights, more to do with lung capacity and the psychology of overcoming the inevitable aching legs. The last two made sure coffee and cake were part of the exercise schedule. Not forgetting Hels Bells and her regular sports massages, which kept me on the road and injury free. All these lovely friends, and more, came to cheer me along on the big day. I can't tell you what a massive boost to my energy levels it was to see them all at various places around the course. Emotions overwhelmed me part way round, trying to steal my breath and make me walk, but then I remembered the reason I was there and who I had lost. I gritted my teeth, pushed on, and felt on top of the world when I crossed the finish line.

Going from a non-runner to completing 13 miles in a year gave me a renewed kick of confidence. In fact, over the past 12 months, I feel I have turned a significant corner, emotionally. Perhaps experiencing Chloe's grief and loss, albeit at a distance, has allowed me to re-process everything that happened to me and Ian 10 years ago. I feel stronger and happier with who I am. I feel optimistic about the future, too. It's as if I've shed a skin and, like a snake, I'm emerging with renewed energy and hopefulness, ready for the next phase of my life.

.

Chapter 40
What does the future hold?

I look back out across the water and take a deep breath. Mole, sat beside me, snuggles into my side, sheltering from a brisk breeze that briefly whips up the water and ruffles his fur.

Never did I imagine I would be writing a book about widowhood, let alone think I would be the one widowed. Then again, I didn't expect to marry, either.

Ian was my life, my best friend, my soulmate and, having met him, I couldn't imagine life alone. Ian and I shared a bond, something very special which some people spend a lifetime searching for and may never find.

Then, suddenly and unexpectedly, he was taken away, without ever fully living out his dreams.

I had two choices: either give up, curl up in a ball and hide from the world, or pick myself up, dust myself down and live my life to the full in his memory. I chose the latter.

I grew up fast in those first few months after his death. I was a naive 19-year old student when I met Ian and willingly let him take charge of many joint and significant life decisions. Now I had to take full accountability for my existence. Widowhood was a wake-up call and I hope I have become a more responsible, compassionate and less judgemental human being as a consequence.

Throughout my life, my love of animals, and particularly horses, has been my saving grace. Horses have been a continuous thread, weaving their charm through my existence. As a child, the riding school provided a sanctuary from school bullies and exam stress. In adulthood, eventing gave Ian and me a shared passion and a lot of fun, not forgetting the opportunity to write. During his illness, the prospect of seeing Moose and riding him motivated Ian to get out of bed when he was fighting the biggest battle of his life. These beautiful, graceful, sensitive creatures continue to be at the very core of my being as I piece together my new future. When I'm with my horses, or my dog, out in the fresh air and countryside, I feel a sense of belonging. I'm a country girl, through and through.

As I write this, I am enjoying life as a single, independent woman. I won't lie; loneliness is still a visitor, despite my network of incredible friends and my furry companions. It's the absence of someone to do nothing with that stirs up a feeling of solitude. However, this period of singledom has served its purpose, giving me time to discover who Kathryn White really is, and learn what boundaries I need to put in place to honour my existence, so I don't lose my identity within any relationship.

Now that I feel stronger and more in tune with who I am I feel ready to meet someone to share the rest of my life with, in time. I trust in the Universe to unite me with the right person as and when the time is right.

Meanwhile, here I am, living my childhood dream with my horse, dog and cat – we will let the canary fly free – making a living doing what I love, writing.

As I sit on the edge of the reservoir, I feel the Reiki energy flowing through me, from my crown to the very core of my being. My eyes have a soft focus as I concentrate on my breath: my rhythmic steady breath; the subconscious reflex of life. Birdcall and the odd bleat of a sheep punctuate the stillness and then my stomach rumbles in protest, bringing me back to the here and now.

Time to go.

I turn to look at Mole, who has curled himself up tightly beside me. Aware of my gaze, he lifts his head.

"Coffee?" I ask. "Shall we find some coffee and cake?"

He cocks his head to the left and then right as I speak, giving the impression he understands every word. I smile and take one last glance at the scenery around us.

My mantra as I move forwards is to go with the flow, to trust my instincts and allow the Universe to guide me.

Life is fleeting. Life matters. And I intend to live mine to the full.

"Rest in peace, my darling Ian. I truly hoped when I began this diary that you would be given the chance to live. That wish was never granted and you were cruelly taken from us. Stay with me, my beautiful man, in my heart and spirit, always."

About the Author

Kathryn lives in the beautiful Chiltern Hills with her horse, dog and cat. She runs a successful medical writing business, Cathean Ltd, to support the development, approval and marketing of new medicines for healthcare companies around the world.

An equestrian journalist for 10 years, Kathryn has written articles and online content for equestrian businesses and magazines.

Photo courtesy of Candice Pottage Photography

When she's not wordsmithing or horse riding, Kathryn loves running, playing hockey, catching up with friends over a coffee (and slice of cake) or practising yoga and Reiki.

You can find out more about Kathryn at: www.cathean.co.uk

Join the conversation and share your experiences on our Life Matters Facebook page.